HOW TO RESTORE YOUR
JOHN DEERE
TWO-CYLINDER TRACTOR

How To Restore Your
JOHN DEERE
Two-Cylinder Tractor

Spencer Yost

MBI Publishing Company

First published in 2002 by MBI Publishing Company, Galtier Plaza, Suite 200, 380 Jackson Street, St. Paul, MN 55101-3885 USA

MBI Publishing Company books are also available at discounts in bulk quantity for industrial or sales-promotional use. For details write to Special Sales Manager at Motorbooks International Wholesalers & Distributors, Galtier Plaza, Suite 200, 380 Jackson Street, St. Paul, MN 55101-3885 USA.

Library of Congress Cataloging-in-Publication Data Available

ISBN 0-7603-1055-6

Edited by Peter Bodensteiner
Designed by Stephanie Michaud

Printed in Hong Kong

On the front cover: A 1954 John Deere Model 40 High-Crop, serial number 60229. The Model 40 tractor appeared in the 1953, 1954 and 1955 John Deere product lines. High Crop production did not start until 1954, but continued through 1955. During these two years, 294 High Crop Model 40s were made. This tractor was originally shipped to California and remained in that state until it was brought east to become part of the Tom Teague collection. It was restored by Joey Kline of Kline Restorations.

Bottom left: Installing the piston rings requires a piston ring expander that safely expands the rings without breaking them. A variety of sizes and styles of pistons are used in John Deere tractors.

Bottom center: Pull out the differential bull gear, being sure to catch the bearing behind it.

Bottom right: Rich "Bud" Johannsen of Lost Art Body and Paint has hung the hood of a Model 520 in his painting booth, where he applies the necessary sealers and paint coats to produce a flawless finish.

On the back cover:
Top: Another view of a 1954 John Deere Model 40 High-Crop.

Bottom right: When replacing brake pads, it is necessary to remove of the heads of the rivets that secured the old pads.

Bottom left: Attach the carburetor's throttle-shaft plate with new screws. The throttle shaft should now turn easily and freely without binding.

Author bio: How to Restore Your John Deere Two-Cylinder Tractor is the third book written by Spencer Yost on antique tractors. He also created the first and the largest web site in the Internet for antique tractors, http://www.atis.net. When not at work at his software company, Piedmont Systems, Inc., he can be found in his shop working on one of the five tractors in his collection, including a 1951 John Deere MT, or his 1957 3/4-ton Chevrolet pickup truck.

Contents

"The complaisant and affectionate nature of very complicated and very simple machines, like the tractor or the linotype, for example, induced him to reflect that the good in mankind was so contagious that it infected metal."
—*Vladimir Nabokov*

DEDICATION

To the memory and legacy of my father, William Yost, and to my mother, Vivian Yost, for never doubting I could live up to either.

ACKNOWLEDGEMENTS

"I not only use all the brains that I have, but all that I can borrow."
—*Woodrow Wilson*

This is my third book, so I am getting to be an old hand at writing books. During this project, there was nothing that occurred that surprised me. The writing, the photography, the process of layout and publishing all seemed familiar and comfortable. With every book I write I am, however, pleasantly surprised anew with the willingness, cooperation and generosity of the folks that I meet during the project. This well of cooperation runs deep and renews my faith in people every time. I want to thank these folks here:

Lou Spiegelberg of Spiegelberg Restorations. On three separate occasions he put up with my cameras and my pesky meddling in his work. In a production shop that requires progress to make money, these intrusions are no small favor. Three thanks to Lou and his wife and family for their hospitality and help with this book.

Robert Beaver of Robert's Carburetor Repair. Robert hosted me on two separate days to photograph his carburetor and magneto rebuilding procedures and facility. In addition to general restoration and repair, Robert's video training products and performance carburetors are well known and enjoyed across the world. I interrupted his work schedule for several hours and never once did he tire of my demands or presence. Robert was open and gracious and I am thankful for his, and his company's help.

Doug Burrey of Burrey Carburetor Service. Doug and his wife hosted me one day while I followed along during two carburetor rebuilds, photographing the company's work. Doug and his staff were gracious and friendly at every turn. In addition, Doug showed me his wonderful collection of rare, old John Deere carburetors—a real treat that I appreciated.

Fred Schroeter of Central Fuel Injection. Fred spent a long morning showing me the ins and outs of diesel fuel injection systems and their restoration. Fred and his staff, like the other companies I mention here, know more about their area of expertise than most of us even suspect is possible. I now know why they have long been considered the standard for professionalism and thoroughness in diesel fuel injection system rebuilding. His mammoth inventory of NOS parts is held in *aircraft hangers*.

Rich "Bud" Johannsen of Lost Art body and painting. Bud allowed two interruptions in as many days so I could photograph his phenomenal body and paint work.

Joey Kline of Kline Restorations. Joey's shop is close to my home and is one that I have had a lot of experience with. He has restored several tractors for friends and acquaintances, and his work is as good as it gets. Naturally, I called him as soon as I was contracted to create this book and he was willing to help. His work shows up in several areas in this book and I am grateful for his help and hospitality. He restored the tractor that appears on the cover of this book.

Herb Neilsen of Neilsen's Spoke Wheel Repair. Herb spent the better part of an afternoon with me and was generous and patient. He taught me more about spoke wheels than I had ever hoped to know. He also took the time to show me his collection of John Deere Bs, and patiently explained all the nuisances and differences between them.

Gary Uken of Uken Restorations. He hosted me on two separate days to answer questions and to photograph his work. He also provided several photographs included in this book. Gary's strong reputation is supported by his quality work and his regular articles in *Two-Cylinder* magazine.

Mike Williams. Mike is a master machinist with a lifetime of experience. After meeting Mike and photographing his work, I realized that while some people are good machinists, some are magicians with metal. Mike is a magician. If you ever have a broken or worn part, and you can't find a replacement, call Mike. I'll bet he can repair that part to like-new condition.

I also would like to thank Carl Jungmeyer of Jungmeyer Restoration for his willingness to open his shop to this project. His restoration work is legendary, and the fact that I couldn't meet him because our schedules did not coincide was a great disappointment for me. I also was scheduled to meet with Dick Buchwald, an active and well-known John Deere collector and restorer. We had several phone conversations regarding this book but weather and a tight schedule conspired against us. Thanks Carl and Dick for your willingness to help. (Contact information for these companies and people, where applicable, is the appendix.)

Several of my friends and acquaintances were a big help with manuscripts, questions, tools and tractors, appearing in photographs or handling other pressing matters while I concentrated on writing. They are: Brice Adams, Jerry Cox, John Davis, Bill Gannaway, Dave Rotigel, Tom Teague (the tractor on the cover is from his collection), Steve Sewell and George Willer. These are tried and true friends who mean a lot to me. Thanks!

In addition to the shops and people whose restoration projects show up in this book, there is a huge group of people whose help, while not directly related to the process, made the success and completion of this book possible. Especially my "long-suffering" wife, Rita, who knows exactly what a "writing widow" is, and my children Elisha and Parker, who willingly share their limited amount of time with Dad in the midst of a book project. I also would like to thank my business partner, Tom Hires, who manned the helm at our company on numerous occasions while I worked on this project, and my editor Peter Bodensteiner and his staff who took a bunch of words and a wad of photographs and finely tuned this work, of which I am very proud.

As I have in every book, I must thank the men and women of Antique Tractor Internet Services, the Web site I run for antique tractors; especially the members of the antique-johndeere mailing list. Their friendship, camaraderie, experience, and knowledge have made me a much better restorer, writer, and person. Their generosity is boundless; I invite you to join us at http://www.atis.net.

The following companies provided materials or permission to reprint materials for this book: John Deere, PPG Coatings, and *Two-Cylinder* magazine. I especially want to thank the John Deere Foundation and Collectors Center for generously providing research materials for this project, and for providing so many resources for collectors across the world.

FOREWORD

"Hell, there are no rules here— we're trying to accomplish something."
—*Thomas A. Edison*

For many people, John Deere Two-Cylinder tractors represent the "best of breed" of antique tractors. They embody many of the traits we associate with fine workmanship and long-term value. The unique engineering, their unique sound, and the lasting designs of John Deere Two-Cylinder tractors create an almost indelible association with the phrase "antique tractor." If you were to ask anyone to draw an antique tractor, he or she would probably draw something that looks like a John Deere GP, an unstyled A, or maybe a styled B, and they would probably color it John Deere green. Unlike many makes of antique tractors, John Deere tractors remain fixtures in the great American landscape. You'll find no other make of antique tractor that generates the excitement and loyalty among collectors such as John Deere Two-Cylinders.

I realize that I am probably preaching to the converted. You picked up this book because you already have, or are considering acquiring, a John Deere Two-Cylinder tractor that needs restoration. Rest assured that this volume will take you through the entire process.

I've included a little advice on purchasing the tractor, and preparing yourself for the restoration process. Then, I take you through restoration, all the way to the finishing touches of decal application. I will cover every major step along the way, including cleaning, mechanical restoration, and painting. You will learn all of the major procedures, and the parts and services you will need to correctly restore a Two-Cylinder. You will also come to understand the need for a realistic and rational schedule to accomplish your restoration project.

Throughout this book I've provided tips and tricks to help you avoid, or at least be aware of, the inevitable "gotchas" that crop up in any restoration project. After reading this book, and reflecting on how it applies to your particular tractor, you will be prepared and ready to restore your own Two-Cylinder.

I wish you the best as you journey through your John Deere restoration project. I am confident this book will become a valuable assistant that will provide help and guidance worth many times its purchase price.

—*Spencer Yost*
January 2002

chapter 1

Getting Started

*"But that two-handed engine at the door stands ready
to smite once, and smite no more."*
—John Milton

There comes a time in almost every tractor admirer's life when he or she thinks about owning, or becomes the owner of, an antique John Deere Two-Cylinder tractor. The sound, the color, the name, and nostalgia all come together to create "green fever," until you finally succumb and decide that *now* is the time to buy and restore one. Once you make this decision, questions begin to overwhelm you: "Which model should I buy?" "What condition should I look for?" "How do I begin to restore it?" "What tools and supplies do I need?" Probably the most important question of all is, "How much is this project going to cost?"

Let's take a little time in this introductory chapter to evaluate the first and second questions. The first step of a restoration project is choosing the right tractor. This is the tractor that will pull at you, motivate you to finish the project, and force you to set goals. The wrong tractor will be left behind in the shed, partially disassembled, and completely forgotten.

This first chapter is also an introduction to the prerequisites needed for a safe and successful restoration. All you really need is space to work, proper tools that will make your effort safe and professional, and a small dash of mechanical know-how that I'll help you acquire. I assume you've had experience with some mechanical basics such as changing oil, troubleshooting, and performing light repairs; that you have at least a general knowledge of how engines and tractors work; and that you know the names of most tools.

The most important prerequisite is preparedness. Being prepared is the result of research and advanced planning. When mixed with desire and dogged persistence, preparedness creates a motivational force that will see you all the way through to the end of a restoration. Conversely, a lack of preparedness and the unrealistic expectations this creates means that few restoration projects are ever completed. The reasons for this are varied. Some are unavoidable, such as financial or health constraints, but most are stalled projects that can be traced to unrealistic approaches when buying the tractor, and when planning the project—approaches that could have been avoided through preparation.

Preparing you, and helping you navigate through a John Deere Two-Cylinder tractor restoration is what this book is all about.

Because a first-class restoration project is an involved undertaking, you should mentally break the project into four broad categories of tasks. They are:
• Research and preparation
• Cleaning and disassembly
• Mechanical restoration and assembly
• Painting and finishing
Accordingly, I have organized the book along these lines. Along the way, I outline procedures and present photographs that are specific to the steps involved, pointing out helpful tips and tricks.

MODEL SELECTION

From tractor engines to power units, the Two-Cylinder engine lived on for more than 30 years in the John Deere family of products. During that time, the engine and its systems underwent notable changes and improvements. Cooling changed from thermosiphon, nonpressurized cooling to pressurized water pump-based cooling; carburetion continually improved over the years; ignitions changed from magneto-based to coil-based; models with diesel-fuel engines were added; and a vertical Two-Cylinder design was added.

Even with these changes, the basic Two-Cylinder-engine design philosophy of John Deere never wavered. The same engine design that powered the early-model Cs and Ds in the 1920s drove every one of the last 30 series built in the late 1950s. Therefore, tractor buffs have a large selection of John Deere models to choose from when considering which antique John Deere to buy.

When you are finished with your restoration, having a like-new tractor leaves you with a tremendous sense of accomplishment, and a great tractor. This tractor was restored by Gary Uken of Uken Restorations, and is one of his personal tractors.

GENERAL CRITERIA

What tractor model, and which particular version of that model should you purchase? I can't tell you what tractor you will like any better than I can tell you what your favorite food is—you have to make that decision yourself.

You may want to try to locate a specific model or a particular tractor that has sentimental value. Obviously, the tractor you buy and restore is a personal choice.

A lot of the disassembly photographs will feature this John Deere 520 tractor. This tractor came to Spiegelberg Restorations with transmission and steering problems, but otherwise was mechanically in good shape.

Tips & Tricks

• If a tractor you are evaluating emits heavy smoke from the exhaust, first note the color of the exhaust, then place a small board or piece of cardboard in the exhaust stream and take a small whiff from the surface. Heavy black smoke coupled with a smell of carbon or gasoline indicates the tractor may need nothing more than a carburetor adjustment. Blue-black smoke with an acrid or "dirty engine" smell indicates significant oil is making its way into the combustion chamber. This presents more of a problem.

MODEL YEARS

I don't list all of the details regarding every model of John Deere—there are several books on the market that do this. But I do give you the names of the books you need for this information in the appendices. Prospective models can be logically grouped into three different year ranges as follows:

EARLIEST MODELS TO MID-1930s

From this time period you can expect nonpressurized cooling systems, nonexistent to very simple hydraulics, the only flathead engines John Deere ever made (though the flathead model LA extends past this timeframe), and very little sheet metal to complicate the restoration. I recommend tractors from this period for first-time restorers. Unfortunately, many of these models tend to be the most expensive, so a little bit of searching may be necessary to find a tractor that is within your price range.

MID-1930S TO EARLY 1950s

Styled sheet metal, pressurized cooling systems, more complicated hydraulics, and other technical improvements raise the bar for the first-time restorer. These tractors can be successfully restored by first-timers, but more work and patience will be required. The late 1940s also mark the introduction of the vertical Two-Cylinder engines, which have many similarities to other familiar engines. Diesel power also was introduced in the model R during this period.

EARLY 1950s TO 1960

This period saw the introduction of the 20- and 30-series tractors. These tractors added much in styling and operator comfort, including two-tone paint, a three-point hitch, and power steering. I recommend that first-time restorers stay away from these tractors unless they have a lot of patience and persistence; these make great second projects.

EVALUATING A TRACTOR

The best piece of advice I can give you about restoring tractors is, "Don't buy problems." Here are criteria to help you avoid some problems. Remember that making decisions about the mechanical condition of a particular tractor has to be done in context. After all, these tractors are more than 40 years old and they are going to have some problems. You must determine the degree of the problems, and if they can be fixed within your budget. After a thorough visual inspection that notes missing parts, the condition of sheet metal, and any other easily visible problems, perform the following tests.

When choosing a tractor, run—don't walk—away from any tractor that looks like this. Its long-term exposure to the weather and missing parts makes this tractor a very poor restoration candidate. It might have some value as a parts tractor, depending on what parts you need, but otherwise, this tractor is gone for good.

The air-intake plenum casting often will have been broken and welded. Pictured here is a typical example of the problem and the usual welded repair. This tends to be unsightly in the finished restoration, therefore, grinding and dressing welds before painting enhances the final appearance. You can find replacement castings at salvage yards if you look hard enough, and don't mind spending the extra money. Gary Uken

ALL TRACTORS

Grab the flywheel of horizontal-engine tractors and try to give it a good shake up and down. Movement means that the crankshaft bearings are heavily worn. This is not a big deal because you probably will be replacing these during restoration, but it's a good test when comparing tractors. Next, try to gently spin the flywheel *without* turning the attached shaft; if the flywheel spins without turning the attached shaft, then the splines on the shaft and/or flywheel are worn. The more the splines are damaged or worn, the more you can free-spin the flywheel. Depending on the amount of wear or damage, this can be a very expensive repair. Anything more than a few degrees of flywheel movement should cause you to rethink whether this tractor is the right one for you.

Steering-wheel free play should be minimal; anything more than a one-quarter turn of the steering wheel, without an accompanying movement of the steering components, indicates significant wear. Excessive play may not be a deal breaker, but all other things being equal, choose the tractor without significant steering-system play.

Structural damage or damage to castings should send up a red flag. Frame members, steering, engine, or transmission castings that show repair should send you on your way empty-handed.

Tires for antique tractors are expensive, and should be in reasonable condition. Because it's unlikely you will use this tractor for anything but show, or for occasional light chores, the tires don't have to be perfect.

The sheet metal should be free of significant damage or rusted-out areas. Bodywork can be challenging, time consuming, expensive, or all three. A tractor with good sheet metal is a much better find than one without.

IF THE TRACTOR IS RUNNING

Listen for abnormal knocks or metallic sounds from the engine, transmission, and hydraulics. Even tractors that are in good condition will create noises in the engine (particularly in the valvetrain) and transmission. None of these noises should have a periodic quality or heavy metallic sound to them. Normal noises that are created by a 40-plus-year-old tractor will be light, constant, and should not skip or have emphasis. Normal transmission noises during movement tend to have a "whirring" quality rather than a "grinding" quality.

Test standard mechanical aspects, such as compression and vacuum. Because you will be restoring this tractor, it's not critical to know the results of these tests when performed on a running tractor. If the tractor starts and runs, you are way ahead of the game.

Test the clutch and try to feel for abnormal play, erratic engagement, or grinding noises during engagement, which would indicate excessive wear or damage. A working clutch will snap when disengaged; a clutch that needs repair won't. The clutch should require moderate force to disengage.

Check the brakes. Look for broken linkages, pedals, and cracked drums on models where the drums are visible. Be sure that evenly placed force on both pedals

Tips & Tricks

• When buying a tractor, especially your first, try to buy one locally whose history you know. A tractor you or your neighbors know something about and have seen in action will be less likely to present you with unpleasant surprises. Plus, you'll incur little if any transportation expense.

stops the tractor in a reasonable amount of time. Brakes are often the Achilles' heel of antique tractors. Typically, because of differential braking during field-work, one side is completely worn while the other side is serviceable.

IF THE TRACTOR IS *NOT* RUNNING

If the tractor doesn't run, does the engine at least turn over? Check to see if the engine is seized by trying the starter. If the starting system doesn't work, or if the tractor manually starts, try to turn over the engine with the flywheel; on the vertical-engine Two-Cylinder tractors, use a wrench on the belt-pulley nut. If it is seized tight, the tractor's rings and pistons are probably rusted or galled to the cylinder walls. If the engine turns slightly but not all the way, then the engine has some other damage such as a broken connecting rod or crankshaft. In this case, see if the seller will allow you to remove the cylinder-head or crankcase cover (oil pan on vertical-engine Two-Cylinders) to inspect as much of the engine as possible. A broken piston may or may not be much of a deal breaker, but a damaged connecting rod could mean more damage such as a bent crankshaft, or heavily scored cylinder walls.

Next, check the running gear of the tractor. If the engine is not seized, tow the tractor slowly on level ground to be sure the brakes and steering are functioning. While being pulled, engage the clutch in all gears to determine any transmission or drivetrain problems. To do the same if the engine is frozen, just leave the clutch disengaged. Try each gear as you test. Although not fool-proof, this test will help expose any serious flaws in the transmission or drivetrain of the tractor.

ESTIMATING RESTORATION COSTS

Estimating restoration costs is dangerous business for authors. For every restoration that I say will cost $5,000, someone will show me how they did it for the grand sum of one swayback mule. Then the next owner/re-storer will tell me I low-balled the estimate because his or her restoration cost twice as much as my estimate. I can give you a few guidelines, in 2002 U.S. dollars. Expect to spend about $5,000 for a very nice, quality restoration to $9,000-plus for a top-of-the-line restoration using original or new-old-stock (NOS) parts wherever possible. If you would be happy with a restoration that is Spartan, giving you a tractor that runs, and a

paint job that is acceptable but not top notch, you can keep your costs under $2,000.

Obviously, your restoration costs will vary depending on many factors. For example, the transmission and hydraulic costs can escalate if you have to chrome shafts or replace all of the bearings. These cost guidelines assume you do most of the work yourself, you want a tractor that looks like new when you are completed, and your tractor came complete with original parts. Another cost factor is whether you take the time necessary to shop for good used parts, and/or if you use new John Deere authentic or NOS parts when necessary.

Tips & Tricks

• Inspecting tires is an important part of evaluating a tractor. Cracks are more worrisome than wear. Don't let significant wear bother you if there are no or minimal cracks. But, be wary of lots of cracks. They are a sign of old, bad rubber, and you will probably have to replace the tires.

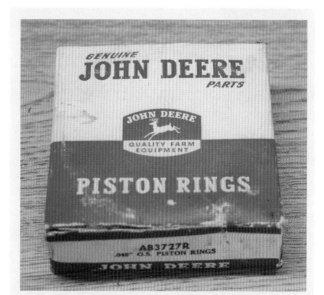

Using N.O.S. (New-Old Stock) parts during your restoration keeps the tractor as original and authentic as possible. Most N.O.S. parts are pricey, but in some cases, such as with these piston rings, the cost is comparable to modern new replacements.

PERSONAL SAFETY

Safety cannot be emphasized enough. I am slightly more emphatic about safety than most, and still have had a few mishaps in the shop myself. Fortunately these mishaps were minor, but they taught me that anyone who spends enough time in a shop will have an accident at some time, no matter how safety-conscious he or she is.

Always use appropriate safety items and tools. Don't use a dust mask when painting—use a paint-fume mask. Use impact goggles when appropriate and splash-proof goggles when needed. Keep both leather and chemical-resistant work gloves on hand, as well as fire extinguishers, first-aid kits, a phone or intercom, and other safety gear.

Use good-quality stands, jacks, and cribs to hold heavy loads. Have a second person available to help or get help when you are doing something dangerous like splitting the tractor in half or lifting heavy, cumbersome pieces. At the very least, have someone check in with you from time to time while you are working on your tractor.

Safety really means keeping these three questions in mind: "Am I thinking ahead and trying to anticipate problems to minimize the likelihood of mishap or injury?" "Am I wearing and using protective gear appropriately, to alleviate the consequences of any injury?" "Am I prepared to treat and resolve any injury after it happens?"

Safety devices are just tools, and memorized safety rules are simply a skill set. None of these are useful unless you are thinking ahead at all times. For example, when doing something as simple as heating a shop, the safety-conscious person realizes shop fumes, such as those created from gasoline and solvent, are drawn into and burned by a space heater. They can produce carbon monoxide in large quantities. You must always provide fresh ventilation in your shop, especially when these and other flammables are present.

Tips & Tricks

• When inspecting a tractor, pay attention to the dents. If the dent depression is shallow, even if it is large, the repair should be straightforward. A deep depression, no matter how small, will probably require patching or significant work to repair.

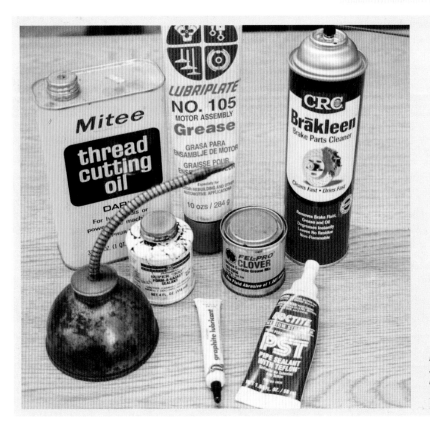

Restoration of mechanical systems requires a few shop supplies. These oils, lubricants, cleaners, sealants, and compounds represent some of the most common ones you use. Other supplies you use a lot are penetrating fluids and anti-seizing compounds.

SHOP SPACE—MECHANICAL AND PAINTING

The minimum space needed to perform the mechanical restoration of a tractor is approximately four times the footprint of the tractor. If your tractor measures 10 feet long by 6 feet wide, you should have at least 240 square feet available for disassembly, temporary storage, tools, and a work area. This doesn't count the long-term storage space needed for large items, such as the hood, wheels, and tires. Your workspace should have good lighting, a concrete floor, and it should offer protection from inclement weather. Heating is optional, but if condensation is a problem in your shop a heated space will minimize rust problems.

The workspace can double as a painting area, but you will need slightly more space if you combine the areas—about six to eight times the footprint of the tractor. There are pros and cons to combining your work and painting spaces. You don't have to shuttle the tractor or parts to a different area, and all of your tools and equip-ment are in one place. But, the overspray from the painting process can get on everything. Plus, dust and dirt left over from the mechanical restoration can affect the paint job unless you keep the area very clean. Using tarps to cover tools, floors, and fixtures will help minimize problems of overspray or dust. Overall, it's best to have two areas—one for painting, and one for mechanical work.

The requirements for a painting area are similar to those needed for the mechanical restoration. In the painting space, adequate lighting and protection from the weather are imperative. I advise having as much sunlight as possible. Heating is necessary if you expect the shop space to reach below freezing; some painting and body supplies and materials cannot be exposed to freezing temperatures. Since most painting tools are air-powered, the painting area must have air-supply lines. Electricity for extra lighting and an occasional power tool also is necessary.

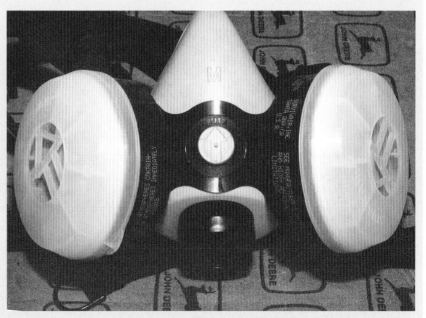

You should never spray paint without wearing one of these. These paint-grade respirators are absolutely necessary to protect yourself from airborne paint and solvent fumes.

A fire extinguisher is a must. With fuel, oil, painting, cleaning, and stripping chemicals in the shop, the risk of fire is great. Always have an ABC-rated fire extinguisher handy.

Tips & Tricks

• When looking for a tractor, try taking out "Wanted to Buy" ads in local periodicals. Many people who have a tractor for sale won't take the time or spend the money to advertise, but will respond to such an ad.

TOOLS

MECHANICAL TOOLS

Doing your own restoration requires a sizable investment in tools. Even if you have a good collection, you'll find new and different tools handy or necessary. For example, you will use a 1/2-inch socket set most of the time, but you also will find a 3/4-inch drive set necessary. In addition, there is a wide variety of specialized tools that will be required during phases of your project. You can rent some, such as cylinder hones, but there are others, such as sleeve pullers, that must be purchased. Or, consider used tools. Used, high-quality tools are preferable to new, cheap tools. You can find high-quality tools at significant savings at yard sales, auctions, or in classified ads.

Here is a small, but certainly not exhaustive, list of tools you will need in your tool collection to start a restoration project. You will need more as you go along, but this will get you started with the disassembly of the tractor.

SOCKET WRENCH SET: You should have a 1/2-inch drive socket set with a good assortment of standard 6-point sockets up to 1 inch. You also will need larger than 1 inch, 12-point, and deep-well sockets from time to time, but you can wait until you need them before acquiring them. You may also wish to purchase a 3/4-inch drive set for large fasteners, and a 3/8-inch drive socket set for small bolts.

COMBINATION WRENCH SET: Combination wrenches are those wrenches with a closed and an open end. A great set of hand wrenches, including a small and large adjustable wrench, is indispensable during restoration.

SCREWDRIVERS: You will need clutch-head screwdrivers in addition to Phillips, and straight-blade screwdrivers, all in multiple sizes.

PLIERS: Have several sizes on hand, from small needle-nosed pliers to large adjustable ones. You also will need snap-ring pliers.

HAMMERS: It's amazing how many times you will use a hammer in restoration. In addition to the specialized bodywork hammers, pictured later in this chapter, you will need a 2-pound mallet, a rawhide or other non-marring mallet, a ball-peen, and a flat-faced (nonserrated) carpenter's hammer.

GENERAL HAND TOOLS: Among the tools you will find useful are measuring tools, including a ruler, dial caliper, ignition and valve clearance gauges, a micrometer, a tap and die set, a pickle fork (to remove steering components), and files of varying lengths.

AIR TOOLS: The only air tool you need to start with is an impact wrench. This will remove most stubborn fasteners quicker and easier than manual tools. You can rent this, but it is needed so often, I recommend buying it.

SHOP FIXTURES AND EQUIPMENT

At some point, you need various shop fixtures to complete certain steps. Again, much of the tools you need can be rented, or borrowed if you have a friend with a well-equipped shop.

AIR COMPRESSOR: An air compressor is a necessity for restoration, as several important power tools and paint application devices are only available in air-powered forms. Some tools and chores require very little air while other chores, such as sandblasting or air-powered sanding, will consume a lot of air. Be sure to match the air-supply capabilities of the compressor to the air-supply requirements of the tools you plan to use.

ENGINE HOIST: This usually can be rented, and is

MECHANICAL TOOLS

In addition to the obvious assortment of handy painting supplies, you'll want a can lid, large and small measuring cups, glazing putty for light final filling of very minor imperfections, a paper strainer to strain paint, and gloves. You also need an assortment of emery paper for sanding out mistakes.

A wheeled tool chest is handy, and about the only way you can keep all of your tools organized and close at hand.

These impact wrenches really come in handy. They make short work of removing stubborn fasteners. If this doesn't do the job, then removal will probably require destructive means. Shown with it are impact grade sockets; regular sockets may shatter and should not be used.

MECHANICAL TOOLS (CONTINUED)

This slide-hammer set is used to remove bearings and bushings, and to pull out dents. A good quality set such as this one is not cheap, but it will save time, it's hassle-free, and it will eventually pay for itself.

Unusual tools that you need include, from left to right: a clutch-head screwdriver (a lot of John Deere sheet-metal fasteners are clutch head), a cotter pin puller, a low profile screwdriver with a socket-wrench adapter, and a cheap screwdriver that you can cut unusual profiles into for the occasional odd circumstance.

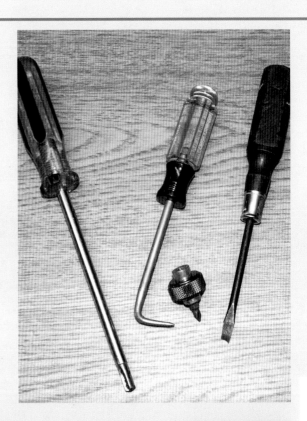

A strap wrench is handy to hold objects, when needed. Here, the strap wrench holds the crankshaft while work is being done on the belt pulley on the opposite side.

Here is a small collection of some of the measuring tools you need. Shown clockwise from the far left are: Ignition gauge, feeler gauge, dial indicator on a magnetic base, dial caliper and bore gauge.

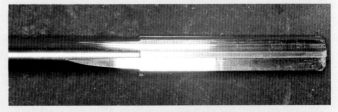

Shown here is the business end of a reamer. These devices are designed to create exceptionally accurate holes in non-hardened metal. They are usually used when reaming bushings. You won't need many sizes, so only buy reamers when you need them.

A requirement for restorations is an electric- or air-powered grinder. This tool will see a lot of work and is useful for grinding off the heads of fasteners and rivets, cleaning up welds, and removing welded customizations.

Some of the tools needed to restore tractors require ingenuity or an unusual method to acquire. A clutch alignment tool is needed when aligning clutch packs on John Deere tractors. This tool was actually available at one time; now, a spare clutch drum with a shaft attached makes a great alignment tool. The drum is available from any John Deere salvage yard.

required for lifting and moving various heavy castings and assemblies.

PARTS WASHER: You don't have to buy this—you can wash parts the old-fashioned way, with a cleaner and a brush over a tub. There are several nice models available at tool supply companies that make washing parts a little less time consuming, and a whole loteasier and safer.

SANDBLASTER: The really large, really rusty components can be taken to a local sandblasting company. But having your own sandblaster–even a small siphon-based system that can be powered by a small compressor–will save a lot of time and hassle when cleaning small parts.

PRESS: Removing press-fit parts makes a shop press necessary. Although some of the heavy-duty pressing may still need to be sent out to a local machine shop, a shop press will take care of most of your work.

WORKBENCH: A workbench is a requirement for restoring small or delicate assemblies like the magneto or carbure-tor, while at the same time providing an anchor for a vise—something that comes in handy during a restoration. Also, a grinder mounted to the workbench or to a separate stand will get used more than a few times during a restoration.

GAS WELDING OUTFIT: Although certainly not necessary, this is handy primarily for heating recalcitrant fasteners (heating them helps to loosen their grip), heating sheet metal to help shape it, and for the occasional brazing job that needs to be done.

MIG WELDING MACHINE: This will be used during cosmetic restoration for patching rusted-out places or fixing cracks, if you plan to do your own sheet-metal restoration. Acceptable, nonstructural MIG welding is learned reasonably fast by hobbyist restorers. If you buy the welder from a welder's supply house, you can usually receive free instruction after the sale. Many of these firms have additional courses available for a small cost. Further instruction is available at local community and trade colleges.

Getting Started

A sandblasting cabinet is tremendously useful. Most folks think of whole tractors and big parts when they think of sandblasting, but the majority of sandblasting work is on small parts. This cabinet will make cleaning small parts quick and easy.

An engine hoist as pictured here, lifts the engine of vertical-engine tractors, and accomplishes general heavy lifting chores for all tractors. Hoists can be rented, as needed.

Few tools are needed for dent repair and sheet metal straightening. These three hammers and dollies will perform 99% of all the dent bumping you'll do. A ball-peen hammer and a few dollies made to match a specific circumstance will round out the body tools.

For heavy sandblasting, a pressure-based sandblasting system, such as this one, is required. A cheaper, smaller, siphon-based system is a waste of time if the piece you're working on is large or heavily rusted. These pressure-based systems are available in a variety of sizes, coinciding with the capacity of sand they hold. Small-capacity units, while somewhat inconvenient, are affordable.

A drill press is used more than a few times during a restoration. In addition to the obvious uses, it also can be used to drill out pins and stuck fasteners.

These are the two paint guns you use the most. The only difference between them is their size. The gun on the left holds a pint, but can be clumsy in tight spaces. The gun on the right holds only 4 or 6 ounces but allows you to paint in the tight spaces.

In addition to the tools mentioned above, the following tools are required for the painting process.

METAL PREPARATION TOOLS

Bodywork is more about patience and technique than tools, but a standard collection of body dollies and special hammers will be necessary for beating out dents and straightening metal. For sanding, body filling, and other general preparation, a dual-action sander is necessary, preferably an air-powered version. Various ordinary chisels, picks, and punches, available at most hardware stores and tool supply houses, will come in handy too.

PAINTING TOOLS

I recommend a high-pressure, low-volume, siphon-fed, air-bleed type of paint gun. Gravity-fed and non-air-bleed guns are less handy to use during painting because of all the odd surfaces that require using the gun at difficult angles. Paint guns are also available in a high-volume, low-pressure (HVLP) version. This type is available as an entirely separate unit with its own compressor, or it can be purchased for use on standard air lines. HVLP technology wastes less paint through overspray, and is friendlier to the environment. More important, its use is required by some states and municipalities. I recommend looking into acquiring an HVLP paint gun if you don't already have a paint gun. The folks at the paint supply houses, or people in the auto body repair business can give you some advice pertaining to your circumstances. A small touchup gun is handy for tight places and, for touching up the paint job during and after the restoration.

These crucial first steps of choosing the right tractor and setting up your shop are important because they help set the tone of the restoration. A rushed and botched tractor buying trip, an incomplete set of tools, a poor workspace, and inadequate information that results from a lack of research will lead to the frustration and mistakes that derail restoration projects. Restoring tractors is about challenging yourself, saving a piece of history, and having fun. Just remember that restoration is a journey, and like any journey most of the fun happens along the way. Enjoy yourself, and now its time to jump in and get some grease under your fingernails..

Loosening Stuck Fasteners

The bane of every antique tractor restorer is the stuck fastener. The following sets of problems and procedures describe working on cap bolts, screws, stud/nut combinations, and so on. I have restored tractors, cars, and trucks, but tractors seem to have more than their fair share of difficult fasteners. The first thing most beginning restorers do wrong is try to use wrenches or screwdrivers too long, rounding off or stripping fasteners in the process.

Early realization that the fastener will require extraordinary means is helpful. Sometimes a nut or fastener just won't come off, no matter what you try. If its proximity to expensive or easily damaged components makes the fastener a poor candidate for grinding, melting, or chiseling, there are several techniques and approaches I use based on the type of fastener involved, and whether I need to save the fastener.

Heat, Oil, and Patience

To use the heat and oil removal method, first clean any threads that are exposed. Place drops of oil at the seam between the fastener and housing or nut. Give the oil a few minutes to penetrate, then heat the fastener—not the housing—if possible. Do not put oil on after heating, as it can harden the bolt and fastener. Try loosening the bolt while it is hot. It will be softer than normal from the heat, so be careful not to use excessive force. If this doesn't work, let it cool completely and try again. If it still won't budge, continue repeating the process until it works. This is where you need a lot of patience.

Drilling

To drill out the fastener, start by choosing a drill bit a few 32nds of an inch smaller than the fastener. Find the exact center of the fastener and mark it on the head with a center punch. Don't be bashful; give the center punch a good whack. This mark will keep the drill bit centered while you start a hole in the bolt. Drilling exactly through the center is important to prevent ruining the threads in the parent housing to which the fastener is attached. Drill slowly, use lots of oil, and keep the bit perfectly centered with the fastener. Eventually you will reach the end of the fastener, and only a few slivers of metal on the threads of the housing will be left. These can be cleaned out with a tap.

SUPPORTING THE TRACTOR DURING RESTORATION

You can support the front end of tractors under the pedestal (here under the Roll-O-Matic housing) for painting and front hub work. It is a safe enough way to support the tractor for short-term work, but it is not safe over a long period of time. The tractor should be supported under the frame, or the front wheels should be installed, and the front of the tractor lowered back to the ground.

To support the rear of the tractor, bolt a suitably sized steel bar to the drawbar-frame mounting holes, then support the bar with jacks. This allows full access for painting. The area under the bar that receives paint is easily touched up once the rear wheels are back in place.

Breaking off the Bolt

Breaking off the bolt is done only when the housing isn't threaded, or when the bolt has only a nut on the other end. Start by placing a heavy hand wrench on the nut or the head of the bolt and then place an appropriate impact socket on the other end. Try to loosen the bolt with an impact hammer, while adjusting the impact wrench to higher and higher torque levels until it breaks the bolt.

Nut Splitters

The nut splitter is an easy tool to use, and can split one or two sides of the nut for removal.   In general terms, this device is a simple steel ring with a sharp wedge on the inside circumference and a bolt opposite of this wedge. By placing the tool around the nut and then tightening the bolt, you drive the wedge into the nut, cutting it open.   You may need to split two sides of the nut before you can remove it.

Melting

Use a welder's gas torch to simply melt away the fastener or the bolt head or nut.

When to Use Each of These Techniques

If the bolt and fastener must be saved, then the oil/heat/patience approach is the only one to use. Any other approach is destructive.

   If the bolt is in a blind hole (bolt in a threaded hole in a casting), drilling is about the only choice after trying the heat and oil method.

   If the bolt head and its nut are accessible, try to break the bolt with a torque wrench if it's a 5/8-inch bolt or smaller. Otherwise, split the nut with a nut splitter.

   If only the nut is accessible, split the nut, or melt it off with a welder's torch. If the nut is not accessible, drill the bolt like it is in a blind hole, or melt the head of the bolt if the conditions allow.

This is the typical way a horizontal-engine tractor is supported during restoration: Jacks under the rear axles with the front end left in place support the front. Single-front-wheel tractors can be unstable in this arrangement if the front wheel accidentally turns. Support the front of these tractors with a crib underneath the front part of the frame.

Supporting the tractor requires good jack stands. Here, the tractor is supported by a block of wood that is held up by the jack stands. Metal-to-metal contact has a low coefficient of friction. Therefore, holding the tractor up directly with the jack stands is actually less safe then the arrangement shown here, when the object being held up has only a flat surface (such as the bottom of the frame) that can rest on the jack stand.

Chapter 2

Initial Disassembly

"The strongest of all warriors are these two — Time and Patience."
—Lee Tolstoy

GENERAL ISSUES

Disassembly is the first big step in your restoration. In the rush and fever of a new project, it's easy to start tearing into the tractor without first preparing yourself, your tractor, and your workspace. Before taking a wrench to your tractor, be sure you have considered the three Rs: readiness, research, and repair.

READINESS: Do you have your workspace prepared, and have a decent set of hand tools ready? Is safety equipment in place? If basic tools and safety equipment are not in place before you start, the temptation is great to improvise, often with dangerous effect. There is a saying, "When all you have is a hammer, all problems start looking like nails." Using the wrong hand tools damages parts and tests your patience. When you don't have the right size wrench, don't be tempted to bring out the vise grips. Likewise, a bucket of water is no substitute for a fire extinguisher. Be sure you have all of the basics covered before beginning disassembly.

RESEARCH: Do you have the necessary operators manuals, service manuals, and historical information about

the tractor? The appendices in the back of this book can steer you to some good sources for these manuals and books. Acquire and familiarize yourself with this documentation before you start.

REPAIR: If the tractor wasn't running when you bought it, can you repair it to the point it will run? You'll want to do this (if the repairs and work are not too extensive, of course) to expose any flaws in the tractor that may need to be addressed during the restoration.

I once bought a tractor that didn't run well. After rebuilding the carburetor it ran well, and allowed me to take it on a few test runs. These tests revealed a hydraulic system that was stronger than the previous owner had described, so I was able to save the considerable expense of hydraulic restoration that I would have performed had I not first gotten the tractor running. Conversely, the steering system turned out to be in worse shape than I thought, so I modified my restoration plans accordingly. Other systems, such as power steering and clutches, are tough to evaluate unless the tractor is running.

INSPECTING AND ORGANIZING PARTS

As you begin disassembly, get in the habit of cleaning and inspecting each part or assembly as you remove it. Make a mental note, if not an actual list, of the work each part may need. These notes will you help plan and pace the progress of your restoration. Although this seems a bit trivial, I think it's frustrating to find myself on the home stretch of the restoration (assembly of the tractor) only to be halted by an expensive or

time-consuming repair or replacement that I didn't catch when I disassembled the tractor.

Whereas the need to replace a part is obvious in most circumstances, I am commonly asked how to recognize when a part or assembly is worn enough to warrant repair and restoration. I recommend you check for three things when evaluating a part: originality, structural integrity, and operation.

If the originality of your finished project is important to you, then all nonoriginal parts and systems should be removed and replaced with original parts and systems. Decide if the part lacks the structural integrity or strength to perform its job because of heavy rust, damage, cracks, or modification. Heavy rust means different things in different circumstances. For example, heavy rust on a wheel rim is typically a bad thing, whereas heavy rust on a simple hidden bracket may not be. You'll have to be the judge, but if you are in doubt, restore the assembly or replace the part.

When checking the operation of the assembly or part, verify that the part moves with the snugness original engineering would dictate. A simple rod passing through a bracket may have been fairly loose even when it was new, but highly engineered components, like assemblies with bearings and bushings, should have very little or no discernable free play, roughness, or periodic noise to their movement when operated by hand. If they do, replacement or repair is in order. A careful examination and common sense coupled with your goals for the project will guide you through part inspection.

Tips & Tricks

• Never throw away a part. If you are going to replace it, keep it for comparison with the new part to verify proper fit. Ordering or receiving the wrong part is very common in equipment restoration. In addition, you can donate the parts to local 4-H, Future Farmers of America (FFA), or other rural organizations because they occasionally restore tractors as projects.

INSPECTING AND ORGANIZING PARTS

Gauges need to be restored, too. Typically, the tachometer, shown on a Model 60 LP tractor, is non-functional. The gauge restoration companies listed in the appendix can restore yours or set you up with refurbished gauges.

Original wiring for most Two-Cylinder John Deere tractors was lacquer-coated braided cloth with soldered connections and rubber insulators. An original restoration will install identical new wiring. The vendors in the appendix can help you with complete harnesses and supplies for creating your own.

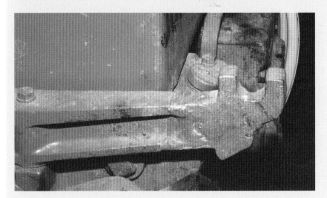

When disassembling, keep an eye out for damage that has been repaired and may need additional work or re-repair. This arm was broken and welded; the welding job was solid and looks good, but a slight touch-up with a grinder will ready the arm for paint.

Initial Disassembly

The brass water manifold that enables water injection is seen on older tractors. They were used to reduce pre-ignition, and to even burning rates when tractor fuel was used, thereby increasing power. They are reproduced and repaired by a few shops across the country. Mike Williams' company, listed in the appendix, is the best place to start.

This is a spoke flywheel of an early Model D John Deere. These are very rare tractors, and when you find them for sale, they often have cracked flywheels that were replaced or repaired by earlier owners. Original flywheels are all but impossible to find, (smaller, 24-inch flywheels are being reproduced) and repair is your only option.

Most tractors have some type of customization left behind by previous owners. Fortunately, this piece was just bolted on so removal is easy; but others are often welded and need a torch and grinder for removal.

You may come across a few clutch-head fasteners. These require special screwdrivers for removal, that are available through some auto parts stores and full line tool houses, or some of the restoration supply shops mentioned in the appendix.

Tips & Tricks
• Used empty paint cans and coffee cans make great containers for storing the byproducts of grease and paint scraping.

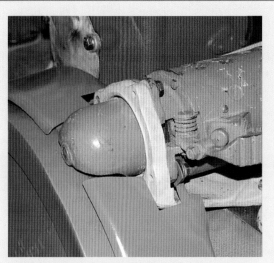

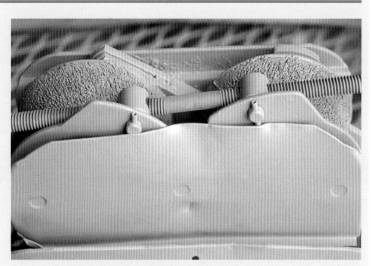

During disassembly, you should verify the authenticity and originality of your tractor's components and parts. Here is a Model A
with an electric starter from a Model AR that was retrofitted to
the tractor. Of course, if originality isn't your goal, and spinning a
flywheel to start your tractor is not your idea of fun, this is an
easy modification to make to your tractor.

Here is a seat shock absorption assembly of a Model 520. These rubber torsion seat springs
(the two round parts seen here) are in need of replacement. It is easier to sandblast and
prime the seat assembly if new springs are installed afterwards.

ORDER OF DISASSEMBLY

Although disassembly is primarily intuitive, there are a
few things that should be done in the proper sequence.
First, you should at least hose off the tractor to remove
dirt and dust before bringing it into the shop. You will
do a more thorough cleaning later on, so there is no
sense bringing 50 or 70 years of dirt into your shop if
you can help it.

Next, *all* fluids should be drained from the tractor.
Fuel should be drained first (don't forget starting tanks,
too) and stored in safe containers away from the tractor,
or used in other machines—the fuel will be too old to
use in the tractor by the time you finish the restoration.
Leave the fuel lines disconnected or remove them completely at this point. LP (liquid petroleum) gas tanks can
be removed after the main tank shutoff valve is closed. I
recommend having a local propane company drain the
LP tanks, and test them for soundness and refurbishment. They'll be able to advise you about the latest filling valves you may need to install to accommodate the
filling equipment found at today's propane stations. If
you plan to fill the tractor from an LP tank you own,
they can also train you on safe filling procedures.

Drain all of the other fluids including hydraulic fluids, being careful to keep coolant away from pets and
children. Remember that crankcases hold incredible
amounts of oil; check your service manuals for capacities. Typical oil drain pans won't be large enough to hold
the amount of oil in these tractors.

Next, remove all of the sheet metal, as damaging it
is an expensive mistake. Most sheet metal can be removed easily, but to remove hoods on many John Deere
Two-Cylinder tractors you'll need to remove the steering
wheel and steering shaft first. The wheel will often be a
real bear to get off. If you need to save the steering
wheel, use a steering-wheel puller, penetrating oil, heat,
and patience for removal. If the steering wheel is damaged beyond repair and requires replacement, you can
cut a kerf through the hub of the steering wheel with a
hack or reciprocating saw. This will release the grip and
allow a puller to remove it.

If your steering shaft is an over-the-hood type, you
can remove the shaft by one of two methods depending on
whether the tractor has power steering. If there is no power
steering, you can remove the shaft by first removing the

nut at the front end of the shaft, under a cover plate. Turn the shaft to "unwind" it from the steering box. If your tractor has power steering, the shaft is coupled to the power-steering power unit. There is a bearing housing that has to be loosened and slid up and out of the way (refer to the photographs), and then a pin that has to be driven out to uncouple the shaft. After the shaft is removed, you have free access to the rest of the sheet metal.

On most unstyled tractors, removing the gas tanks and hood is straightforward. The fuel line should still be disconnected from the draining procedure; simply loosen the mounting straps or bracket fasteners, and the tanks and hood will come right off. On styled tractors, the hood supports the tank, so the best way to remove it is to first remove the hood from its supports and then remove the hood and tank as an entire unit. On diesel-engine tractors, you should now remove all fuel filters and fuel lines that lead to the fuel pump and metering assembly.

From here, I like to start at the rear of the tractor and move forward. There is no need to disassemble the hydraulic lift system in any significant way at this point; any lift arms, linkages, or auxiliary hydraulic hoses that were left on the tractor should be removed now. Previous owners of the tractor may have customized the tractor with steps bolted to axles, top link holders, extra toolboxes, or other added features. Any customizations that will get in the way of painting or restoration should be removed at this point. Unfortunately, you will find that many of these customizations are welded, and nothing but a grinder or torch will remove them.

Next, remove the operator's seat. On some models with an electric start, the operator's platform/seat assembly houses the battery. The battery usually has rusted the bottom of the seat platform, so care must be taken if you want to save the platform. The fasteners at the bottom that attach the platform to the transmission case are often impossible to remove. Carefully grind off the head of the fastener and drill out the remainder of the bolt after the seat and platform are out of the way. While removing the seat and platform, hydraulic lines

can be in the way and may need to be removed to prevent damage. Older style, pan-type seats can be removed as an entire unit. Simply remove the bolts that attach the support arm and spring bracket to the transmission case. Removing the pan seat, with its heavily rusted fasteners, is easier when the unit is off the tractor.

The remainder of the initial disassembly includes steps to remove the front dash, wiring, and implement lifts. The front dash disassembly is straightforward, but remember that the gauges should be removed first and care should be taken in removing fasteners because they, and the dash sheet metal under them, tend to be heavily rusted if the tractor has seen much rain. Drilling out these fasteners may be your best bet if it looks like some damage to the dash may occur when applying more conventional methods.

The tractor's wiring can be removed at this point. If the wiring isn't a complete rat's nest, it will be helpful during disassembly to tag each end of each wire as you remove it, noting its location and purpose. This is true even if you plan to make your own wiring or buy a new wiring harness. Address labels folded in half over the wires work great for this purpose.

Now you are ready to remove the electric starter and generator and any auxiliary engine systems. If your John Deere tractor is a diesel with a pony starter motor, now is the time to remove the pony motor. The motor engagement linkages will need to be removed first. Next, loosen the exhaust gas bypass manifold and then remove the fuel lines. Place the pony motor on a bench for rebuilding.

Remove the cooling system components from the tractor engine, such as the radiator, radiator inlet and outlet pipes, and hoses. Then remove the cooling water pump and the auxiliary drive shaft (horizontal engines only). If a power-steering system exists, disconnect the hydraulic lines and cap the ports they were attached to, then remove the hydraulic pump from its mounting.

Tips & Tricks

• Egg cartons make great organizers for groups of large fasteners. They are easy to mark and stack, and the small holes in the top make it easy to see what's inside without opening.

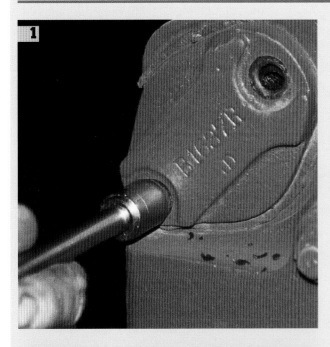

To remove the steering-wheel shaft you must first remove the steering wheel. Then you remove the worm bearing housing shown in the first photograph. After this has been removed, twist the steering wheel shaft out of the sector gear and pull the shaft out. Restoration of the steering wheel and shaft usually includes a new worm bearing, steering wheel shaft support bushing, and recovering of the steering wheel. Often, the shaft itself also needs to be straightened.

(left) This steering-shaft support bushing is shot and needs replacement. This is a common problem on most John Deere tractors that need restoration.

Here is the power steering pump and hoses. Disassembly starts by draining the power steering fluid and removing the hoses. Dirt can create serious problems with any hydraulic system; be sure to scrape off the excess dirt from around hydraulic ports and connections. After removing the hoses, plug the openings on the tractor (photo 6) with hydraulic port caps to keep the dirt out.

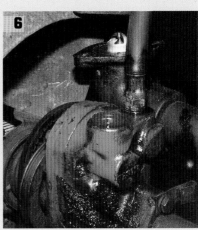

Initial Disassembly

To remove the steering shaft on a tractor with power steering, uncouple the shaft from the steering valve sleeve. Originally, a spring pin was used to couple the shaft, but wear and a few shaft removals result in what you see here: a small bolt and nut instead of a spring pin. To make matters worse, the pin holes are often wallowed out, creating free play in the steering wheel.

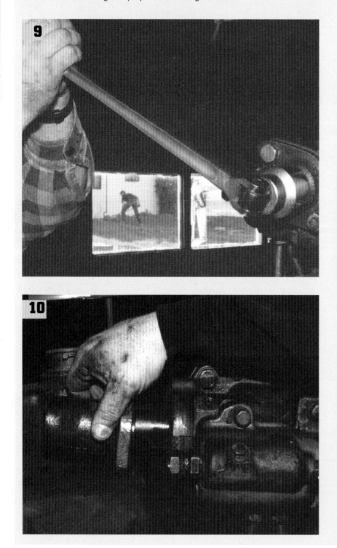

To remove the worm housing from the power steering unit, loosen and remove the plug found at the back of the unit (9). Continue by removing the steering-shaft oil seal housing, (a notorious place for leaks to develop)(10). Then, re-move the worm housing. When doing so on tractors with power steering, make an index mark (11) This will help you set the worm-sector gear lash to its current specification when installing the unit. Further adjustment can be done through the rear plug hole during installation.

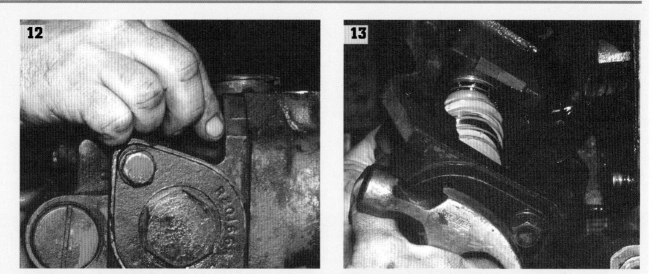

When the shaft is uncoupled and an index mark is punched, removing the worm gear housing is as simple as removing the mounting bolts. Be ready to catch the unit as it comes off the tractor (13).

Removing the hood of styled tractors requires detaching the brackets from the tractor. Although it's intuitive to detach the brackets from the hood, it's much easier to detach the brackets from the tractor, as Lou Spiegelberg shows.

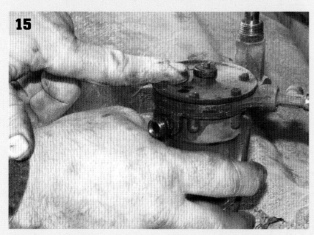

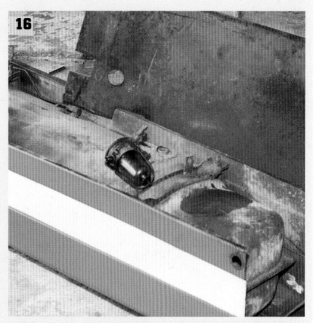

All fuel is drained from the tractor before disassembly. After draining, cut off the fuel so that any small amounts remaining in the tank won't spill when you take off the hood. The fuel cut-off knob is being pointed out here.

Remove the fuel tank after the hood is removed; remove the fuel strainer bowl before starting.

A TYPICAL DISASSEMBLY (CONTINUED)

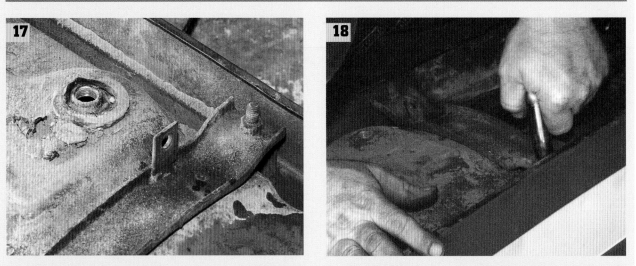

To remove the gas tank, loosen the hood/tank-mounting bracket from the straps that secure it to the tank. These four photographs show the necessary steps.

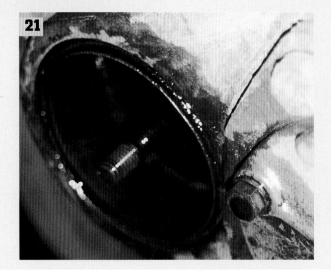

To remove the oil filter you must first remove the oil filter bottom. After removing the single bolt, pull the bottom off and the filter element out. The body, inside the main case, can be removed later during engine work.

Getting Organized

Although I am not the most organized person in the world, I find the following items very helpful during a restoration to keep parts organized and safe:

- *Locking plastic bags*
- *Small- and medium-sized boxes*
- *Tags with a string or wire attached*
- *Permanent markers (to label bags and boxes, but also to mark directly on the part if needed)*
- *Whiteboard*

These all can be found in office supply stores. I store nuts and bolts in old library card catalog cabinets. These cabinets have lots of strong drawers that can take the weight of fasteners, plus they have a holder on the front that can hold a descriptive label. You can find them at surplus and antique stores. Any extra effort to safely store and organize parts will save time and money.

Tips & Tricks

• If originality is important to you, you should save samples of the old wiring harness, even if it's nearly shot. Keeping samples of the wire will allow you to match replacement wire by insulation type, color, and size, and will allow you to reproduce the style and technique of attaching terminal ends.

Before removing the oil pump, remove all of the oil lines from the pump body, accessed through the crankcase cover. Then, remove the oil-filter mounting plate found at the bottom of the tractor, and simply pull the entire unit. Model H tractors must first have the oil pressure regulating screws adjusted all the way in.

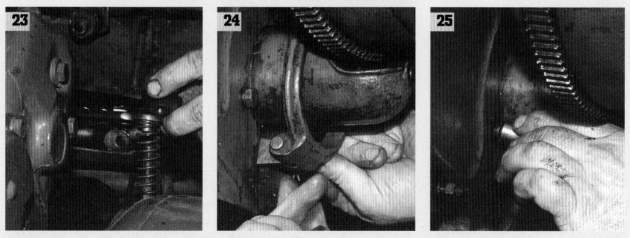

Removing the starter from later-model horizontal-engine tractors begins with removing the starter access cover under the tractor. Then, unscrew the foot catch of the starter linkage, shown, being sure to hold onto the spring and bushing (23). Next, remove the flywheel cover by removing several bolts. Then, remove the linkage yoke from the starter, shown here attached to the starter with a pin kept in place with a cotter pin (24). The starter's mounting bolts can then be removed (25), and the starter lowered out of the tractor.

Initial Disassembly

To remove the generator, simply loosen the bolt that adjusts the tension on the drive belt, then remove the mounting bolts at the bottom of the bracket. You can then lift the unit off the tractor. It's best to have the generator and starter restored professionally.

To remove the front cowl, you must remove two bolts, one on each side, as shown. These are tough fasteners to get off and are often stuck; notice the dents and dings in the cowl, caused by wrenches that have slipped, or over-anxious mechanics. Socket wrenches won't fit so use an offset combination wrench. Care and patience will keep you from repeating the same damage as a previous owner.

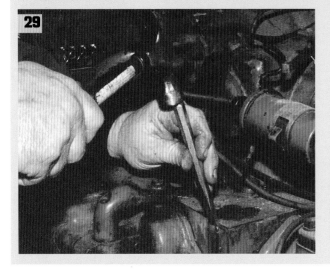

Sandblasting and painting a tractor without damaging the serial number plate is difficult; it's best to remove it. Start by chiseling off the rivet heads (29); the correct angle and a deft touch will shear it off without leaving a scratch on the plate. After removal, carefully drill and chip out the remainder of the rivet from its blind hole. Remember not to damage the hole or new rivets may not hold! Shown far left is a new rivet from John Deere. Installation simply requires that you use a small rivet punch and hammer to drive the new rivet home.

After you remove the cooling tube and connecting hoses, remove the water manifold (shown) from the engine. This will give the coolant cavities in the block a chance to dry out and allow you to inspect the block and coolant-water manifold for freeze cracks.

To remove the water pump, remove the lower coolant tube and connecting hoses, then simply unbolt it from the radiator.

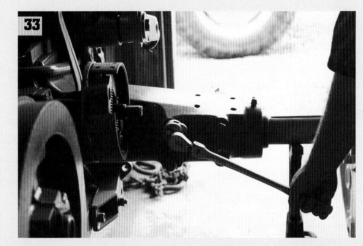

Removal of studs requires the use of a stud extractor. In this photograph, the implement-attachment studs are being removed. Replacing the studs is recommended. However, if the studs come out easily, they can be reused if you clean up the threads with a die after reinstallation.

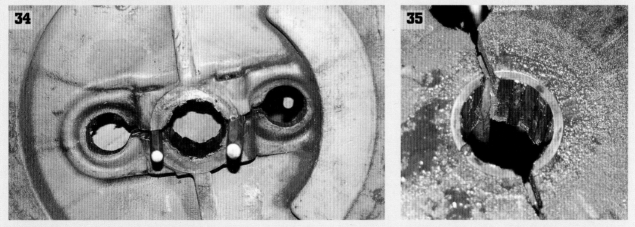

Theoretically, you can remove the flywheel by hand after the hub bolts have been loosened. Usually the flywheel requires a bit of persuasion, though. You can see wedges driven into the hub cutaway, to break the flywheel loose from the crankshaft (34). Then, you can usually pull the flywheel off without much trouble. Remember: these things are heavy, so have a helper ready.

Cleaning Parts

What do I do when I clean a part? First, I send large castings and other difficult-to-handle parts to a commercial sandblasting facility for cleaning. Their large, industrial sandblasters will also burn off grease and grime, something my home shop equipment can't do. For all other parts, I first decide if the part will be cleaned in the course of other outside work. For example, cylinder heads that will be surfaced are almost always cleaned by the machine shop that does the work. Likewise, generators and starters are usually cleaned, primed, and maybe even painted by the shop that rebuilds it. There's no sense in cleaning it myself if it will get cleaned elsewhere. If a part won't be cleaned elsewhere, I soak the part in lye solution to remove the paint as well as the grease and grime. Then, if stubborn paint or the existence of rust dictates, I sandblast the part. After this type of cleaning, a part will start rusting almost immediately, so I coat it with oil or prime it right away after this heavy cleaning.

TRACTOR CLEANING

We are waiting until this stage of disassembly to start the first thorough cleaning. You will be able to reach and clean almost all places on the tractor. To begin, simply ferry the tractor and all of the parts that have been removed so far to a suitable spot outside your shop. Before cleaning, close off openings that shouldn't get water in them—such as hydraulic lines, manifolds, oil lines, and crankcase and belt-pulley openings—with duct tape and heavy plastic. Be sure to cover and seal the magneto or distributor with heavy plastic and copious amounts of duct tape. You definitely don't want water in these items.

You can clean the tractor by hand with a strong cleaner, wire brush, and water, but most prefer to use a high-pressure steam cleaner to complete this step. A high-pressure steam cleaner will remove virtually all grease and dirt from the tractor. Some of these washers may be available with a sand feeder attachment, which is designed to perform some light sandblasting and ensure that the tractor is as clean as possible. This attachment isn't necessary at this point, but feel free to use it if you think it will help in your circumstance. Note that some items, such as the radiator core, can be cleaned with a pressure washer, but at a lower pressure setting (its fins can sustain damage at high pressure).

After a general cleaning, systems and parts can be removed from the tractor as you rework them. For example, the engine can be disassembled when you are ready to rebuild it. The steps for these phases of disassembly are included in the sections that address the mechanical restoration.

As you refurbish and restore parts and systems, they will need to be thoroughly cleaned, including removing rust and stripping off old paint. This is the nasty, tedious work of any restoration. The new paint you'll apply requires a sound, immaculate surface to adhere properly. Skimping on surface preparation will show in the finished project, and lower the expected life of your restoration project.

Two primary methods are used to prepare surfaces, mechanical abrasion and chemical stripping. Each method is suited to a particular set of circumstances.

When it comes to rust, sandblasting is the only process that works with any speed or efficiency. Sandblasting and other forms of mechanical abrasion create immense quantities of paint dust that may contain lead and other heavy metals, which you should not be exposed to. Mechanical abrasion is best accomplished when the dust can be contained, such as in a sandblasting cabinet. Be sure to always wear a dust mask, and shower off all paint dust after each work period. Most sandblasting equipment that is available through home improvement stores and farm shops is not powerful enough to burn grease and grime off the tractor, Here, you will have to chemically clean surfaces to remove the grease and grime first.

Chemical strippers won't remove rust, but they will remove most old paints, grease, and oil. There are three categories of chemicals used during chemical stripping: solvent-based strippers, lye-based strippers, and "safe strippers" (most are under patent and their contents are unknown, but I understand these are compounds of biological origin).

Solvent-based strippers are the most familiar and can be found under various brand names at hardware stores. These work reasonably well, but contain a dangerous chemical known as methyl ethyl ketone that must be handled carefully with complete ventilation, a respirator, and gloves. The drawbacks are many. The resulting residue that must be scraped from the part is an amalgam of dangerous chemicals and lead paint—a nasty combination that requires special disposal. In addition, removing all traces of the stripper from the tractor is very important because your new paint job won't adhere if any residue remains. This seems to be an especially difficult problem around gaskets and seams, where the stripper seems to leach out for quite

some time and cause the new paint to soften and bubble. Cleanup of the stripper can be done with lacquer thinner, and also requires complete ventilation, a respirator, and gloves to apply, plus, it's highly flammable.

The second category of chemical strippers are lye-based strippers. Most are known as some type of "purple cleaner." When you need to strip paint from a vertical surface or a very large part, use a foaming oven cleaner, which is nothing but lye cleaner in foam-based form. The lye will soften the old paint after just one or two applications. Then the paint and grime can be scraped off and placed in a sealable container. For other parts, it's easy and inexpensive to make your own lye cleaner: mix a solution of three ounces of lye to each gallon of water. This solution is also great for removing sludge and grease from parts. Cleaning the residue of the lye from the parts is as easy as washing them with water. Adding some vinegar to the rinse water neutralizes any residue.

Removing paint and rust with lye has several drawbacks. Lye-based stripping doesn't affect many new types of paint, so if your tractor has been repainted in the last 10 or 15 years, lye may not strip the paint from parts. Lye will also dissolve many types of nonferrous metals including aluminum and brass, and they should not be exposed to lye for any length of time. This type of cleaner will cause chemical burns on the skin and eyes, so splash-proof goggles and gloves, and full-length clothing and aprons must be worn when using it. The solution and residue, although not as environmentally damaging as solvent-based strippers, still require proper disposal because the residue will contain heavy metals from the grease and paint. When I dispose of it, I neutralize it with vinegar. Then I let it evaporate as much as possible to reduce the amount I must handle and transport to the hazardous waste facility.

Safe strippers are nonflammable and nontoxic and are available at hardware stores. In most cases these do not perform as well or as fast as the other two categories of chemicals, and they are the most expensive of the three. Safe strippers seem to have many of the drawbacks of solvent-based strippers (leaching from joints, etc.).

Regardless of the chemical stripping method you use, all residue removed from the tractor contains paint and grease, and must be safely disposed.

This is a common problem. In this photograph you can see significant wear on the belt-pulley splines of the crankshaft. This also occurs on flywheel splines. The belt pulley will never be tight or run true until these are repaired.

Mike Williams has chucked the crankshaft up to the lathe for repairs. Next, Mike slowly removes the splines over several passes until he reaches metal that has not been hardened by the belt pulley. After this phase, he builds up the shaft through welding, and then turns it down to specification on the lathe. Using special equipment, he cuts new splines in the shaft.

Tips & Tricks

• Pressure washers have been coming down in price and increasing in variety over the last few years. You may want to consider buying one because they are handy for so many other chores around your home and farm, aside from tractor cleaning.

• Always seal the ends of any hydraulic, oil, or fuel line after removing it from your tractor. It's amazing how much dust and dirt works its way into these lines between the time you remove them and reinstall them. Small corks, duct tape or in the case of hydraulic lines - special plugs sold for this purpose, can be used to seal lines.

FINISHING OUT THE INITIAL DISASSEMBLY

If you have a vertical Two-Cylinder engine, now is the time to get the engine stand ready for the motor. Horizontal Two-Cylinder engines don't lend themselves to engine-stand mounting, therefore, an engine stand isn't necessary. On Two-Cylinder tractors that have belt-pulley-mounted clutches, now is a good time to disassemble the clutch to see what kind of shape it is in and what type of work will be needed. Likewise, now would be the time to remove the flywheel. The items that will be sent out for restoration, such as the steering wheel or the diesel fuel-injection units, can be sent to your restorer or stored until you are ready to send them. If you have a John Deere crawler, now is the time to remove the undercarriage and measure the components.

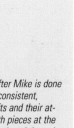

This is the end of the crankshaft after Mike is done turning it on the lathe. Notice the consistent, grainy texture of the steel. As shafts and their attached parts turn, the metal on both pieces at the junction of the two will become hardened through the years from vibration and minute repetitive impacts. This process accelerates as the splines wear; the hardening is called work hardening. Mike removes any metal that shows signs of work hardening. An even, grainy texture indicates metal that has not hardened.

Restoring tractors sometimes means making your own parts. When a part isn't available, a machine shop can usually fabricate a replacement. In these two photographs, a bushing that was nearly the right size is being made to fit its application by the staff at Robert's Carburetor Repair. It will be used as a throttle shaft bushing on an older carburetor.

These are some of the more unusual John Deere parts that are being manufactured new. From left to right: a large valve-spring backer for early Model Ds; magneto coupling; power-steering pump shaft, vanes and vane hub; rope ball for rope-started Model R pony motors; in the center are clutch dog pins. These were all manufactured by Mike Williams.

Mechanical Restoration

"Life is 440 horsepower in a 2-cylinder engine."
—Henry Miller

ENGINE RESTORATION PROCEDURES

Engine rebuilding is an important part of any tractor restoration. It signifies that your project is not just a "clean and paint" refurbishment, but a complete restoration. Unless your tractor's engine has been rebuilt recently, you will want to rebuild it as part of the restoration project. The simplicity of these engines allows even weekend amateurs the chance to rebuild them successfully. Although this book covers the important aspects and nuances of John Deere Two-Cylinder engine rebuilding, it is beyond the scope of this book to cover every possible procedure,

outcome, or consequence that is common to any engine. For this reason, I recommend you pick up a copy of another book I've written: *How to Rebuild and Restore Farm Tractor Engines.* It goes into the all of the specific restoration procedures that are not included in this book.

Tips & Tricks
• Diesel motor pony engines can be restored following the same advice outlined in this chapter.

REMOVAL OF MAIN COMPONENTS—ALL TRACTORS

Before beginning restoration of the engine, be sure you have followed the disassembly chapter and have removed all of the components from the engine that are not part of the engine restoration, such as the coolant manifold, starter, dash, or any midframe implement mounting brackets or tool bars. Also be sure you have

the service manuals for your tractor on hand and ready for quick reference. Now is the time to give your engine another thorough visual inspection to make sure there is no damage you didn't notice before, through the clutter of parts, brackets, and sheet metal.

ENGINE REMOVAL AND DISASSEMBLY

There are three primary structural configurations of John Deere tractors. The first configuration is an engine and transmission that are, for all intents and purposes, a single structural entity. An example is just about every horizontal Two-Cylinder John Deere tractor. These tractors have a separate frame that supports the front end. In the second configuration, the crankcase is

separate from the transmission and acts as a structural member that supports the front end. John Deere tractors with vertical two-cylinder engines have this configuration. The last is where the engine is separate from the transmission and is mounted to a frame that is the support for the engine and front end. An example of this configuration is the 62/L/LA line. Engine removal of frame-mounted engines such as those found in the 62/L/LA line of tractors is straightforward; you simply dismount the engine from the frame. There are no special considerations or any structural or tractor support issues to consider. You can then place the engine on a stand for restoration.

Vertical engine removal procedures follow the same lines as removal procedures used with engines from other makes of tractors you may be familiar with. That is, you must jack up and support the tractor under the engine and then remove the front axle or pedestal. After removal of the front end, you raise the tractor using a hoist attached to the cylinder head, and then place a support for the tractor under the torque tube (the casting that bridges the transmission and engine). Lower the tractor onto this support(s). With the engine hoist still in place, you can unbolt the engine and pull it away. Be sure to pull it forward from the torque tube in a level manner to prevent the pilot shaft from binding in the pilot bushing or clutch.

You can then mount this engine to a stand for restoration, but first you'll need to remove the clutch and flywheel. To make this a bit easier, you should lower the engine onto blocks of wood to stabilize the engine. Maintain virtually all of the weight on the hoist rather than the blocks of wood to minimize the danger of the engine tipping sideways while you work on the flywheel and clutch. The clutch assembly is attached to the flywheel with bolts; likewise, the flywheel is fastened in the crankshaft flange with bolts. As you loosen and remove the flywheel mounting bolts, have a helper available to hold the flywheel—it is very heavy.

The horizontal Two-Cylinder tractors make use of a frame to support the front end; in addition, the transmission case and crankcase are both part of the same casting. The combined casting is called a maincase. This arrangement allows you to remove the cylinder block and head separately. The model D is one significant exception to this "horizontal engine" rule. This model integrates a front-end support under the cylinder block. A model D will have to be supported under the maincase to remove the front-end support from the cylinder block before the block can be removed. With all horizontal engines, though, there is no need for an engine stand and the block can be placed upright on an impromptu stand made of wood, for further work. Finally, remove the valve cover from overhead-valve engines.

Tips & Tricks

- Never use a gasket sealant on a head gasket.

- Even if your cylinder block and head do not need machining, you may want to consider taking them to a machine shop for cleaning. They have rust- and scale-removing chemicals and washing systems that clean out the coolant cavities of these castings much better than in a home shop.

CYLINDER-HEAD REMOVAL

To remove the cylinder head on John Deere tractors without overhead valves (models C, GP, and 62/L/LA), you'll simply need to unbolt it from the crankcase or cylinder block. Because the valves and valvetrain components are in the block, you can skip ahead to the actual head removal procedures that follow.

For those tractors with overhead valves, you'll want to disassemble the valvetrain components that are mounted to the cylinder head before trying to remove the cylinder head. The valves will remain in the head for now, but you'll want to remove the rocker-arm assembly and pushrods. To remove the rocker-arm assembly, loosen and remove the fasteners that mount the rocker-arm shaft supports to the cylinder head. Usually these are nuts fastened to studs, but they may have been switched to bolts in the past. This entire assembly will then lift out, allowing access to the pushrods. Remove the pushrods and store them in a manner that will allow you to keep track of their original position in the engine. They should be returned to those positions later during assembly if you reuse them. To disassemble the rocker-arm assembly further, loosen the keepers (these vary between snap rings, cotter pins, and set screws depending on the model) and carefully remove each rocker arm and support from the shaft. Again, the ordinal positions of these parts should be noted and maintained while these parts are off the tractor. At this point, you have clear access to the cylinder head.

Mechanical Restoration

To remove the cylinder head, remove all of the nuts from the cylinder-head studs. If the cylinder-head fasteners have been switched to bolts from the original studs, loosen, but don't remove these bolts. Loosen them just a little, about an inch to give the cylinder head enough space to move away from the block when you split the two apart. To split the head from the block, use a putty knife or similar tool between the head gasket and cylinder block. The block and head are not typically stuck together tightly but they do sometimes require a splitting force to separate. Once the cylinder head is loose, you can carefully slide it off the studs. Again, if the cylinder-head fasteners have been switched to bolts from the original studs, be ready for any type of unexpected movement of the head as you remove the last few bolts.

Tips & Tricks

• Cylinder-head studs or bolts should be coated with a thread sealant to prevent the escape of coolant past the threads.

CYLINDER-HEAD REMOVAL

This is a close-up of the valvetrain of a Model 60. Note the two large nuts, each with a smaller lock nut, at the top of the rocker arm assembly. These fasteners will remove the rocker arm from the cylinder head.

Notice the large plug-hole openings on the side near the top of this John Deere H cylinder head. Removal of the rocker arm shaft requires removal of the plugs. First, reduce pressure on the rocker arms by loosening the rocker-arm lash adjusting screws. The shaft can then be pulled through the plug arms.

When you open up your engine, you are likely to see something like this—lots of carbon and coolant cavity rust. Even though it's not much to look at, this Model H engine is actually in good shape. There is no cylinder wall damage, no piston damage, and no cracks between the bores. This engine will restore nicely.

Access to the engine starts with the removal of the crankcase cover. Here, the rod caps were removed (foreground) to determine if a noise suspected to be a rod knock was indeed a knock. It was, and the rod had to be replaced, and the crankshaft ground to repair the damage.

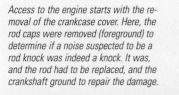

Take a closer look at the removal of the connecting rod cap. This is done first before removal of the cylinder block, rods and pistons so that we can take a rod-bearing running clearance measurement. The top of the crankshaft, part of which is seen in the crankcase here, is in the correct position for removing the caps. From here, you can begin taking the measurement using Plastigage. Note the lighter color found inside the crankcase; to prevent oil from seeping through porous cast iron over the years, John Deere primed the inside of any housing that held fluid.

Model H push rods prevent access to the connecting rods. You must first remove the push rods from the front of the cylinder head before you can get to the connecting rod caps.

Here is an example of some of the bearing problems you'll encounter with an insert-type bearing. The first bearing is worn through to the copper backing, and exhibits significant scoring. The bearing at right shows heat galling, in addition to wear, that made it through to the copper backing. Both will need to be replaced.

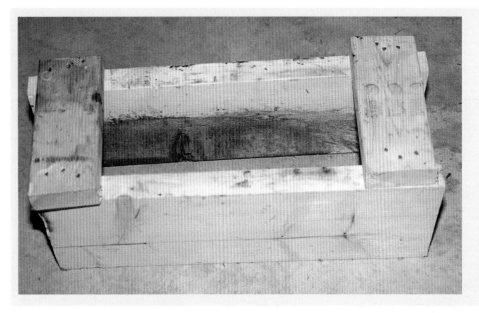

Holding the horizontal-engine cylinder block vertical and elevated during honing and other operations is as simple as building a scrap-wood crib. The crib pictured was made for a John Deere B and from 2x10s and 2x4s nailed together. You'll need larger wood for larger-size tractors' blocks. These cribs are more than sufficient to keep the block steady, and are far enough off the ground to allow clearance and access underneath.

Tips & Tricks

• When lapping valves, water-based valve grinding compound is best and should be used liberally. A wet rag is all that is needed for cleanup to remove all traces of grit.

CYLINDER-BLOCK REMOVAL—HORIZONTAL ENGINES

The following applies to horizontal engines, as the cylinder block and crankcase of vertical engines are a single casting and were removed from the tractor earlier. Before removing the cylinder block, you'll want to take bearing-clearance measurements of the rod bearings. The next section has more detailed instructions on performing this procedure. When the connecting rods are free from the crankshaft, you can remove the cylinder block. This is accomplished by removing the nuts that fasten it to the maincase. Some gentle prying with a crowbar, or pulling with a small winch, anchored to the block and the front end, may be necessary to get the cylinder block free of the frame, mounting studs, and maincase. There is also a gasket between the block and the maincase, so if you are going to make your own replacement gaskets, try not to damage this gasket too much and you can use it as a template for cutting your new gasket. The connecting rods and pistons will come out with the cylinder block.

PISTON REMOVAL AND CYLINDER BORE RESTORATION—ALL TRACTORS

Before you remove the pistons and rods, you should take a clearance measurement of each rod bearing. On vertical-engine tractors, accessing the rod caps is easy when the engine is mounted to the stand, and the oil pan is removed. On horizontal-engine tractors, you will need to remove the crankcase cover and work inside the crankcase. This is the large plate-type cover found on the top of the maincase just in front of where the dash would be. On horizontal-engine tractors, access to the connecting-rod cap fasteners is easier if you turn the crankshaft by hand so that each connecting-rod cap is as close to the top as possible when you work on it. Remove the cotter pins found on the connecting-rod cap nuts. Then, loosen the nuts and remove the connecting-rod cap. Be sure you note the orientation of the cap in relation to the connecting rod. It will have to be installed the same way for the measurement we'll take next, and for final assembly later.

Take a bearing clearance measurement at this time with Plastigage (see the sidebar on page 64). Remove the caps again, cleaning off Plastigage from the bearing and crankshaft. Then slowly rotate the crankshaft to push the piston and connecting rod up into the cylinder block as far as it will go. Repeat the Plastigage measurement for the other connecting rod. Keep these measurements handy for use during the assessment phase of crankshaft restoration. After some additional work, we'll return our attention to the crankshaft, and these measurements will be used then. Once the cylinder block is free from the tractor, remove the pistons that are found in horizontal-engine tractors by grabbing the connecting rod at its bottom, and drawing it and the piston out through the bottom of the cylinder block. If the pistons are stuck in the bore, see the sidebar on freeing up a stuck engine. Vertical-engine restorers will have to use a ridge reamer to remove the unworn landing that exists at the top of the cylinder first, and then remove the piston/connecting-rod assemblies through the top of the engine block.

Remove the piston rings with a piston-ring remover, including any lower oil rings found on the piston. Then remove the connecting rod by removing the clips at the ends of the wrist pins. After the clips are removed, push out the wrist pin, and store together as a set the pin, clips, connecting rod, and rod cap. Clean the piston with cleaner (don't use lye if aluminum replacement pistons are used in your engine) and scrape the piston-ring grooves with a ring-groove cleaner or with the end of a piston ring that you just removed. Piston rings and the knives on piston-ring groove cleaning tools are hard enough to gouge aluminum, so if your tractor has aluminum replacement pistons (originally, they were cast iron), be sure to clean the grooves carefully.

To refurbish the pistons and bores, first take accurate measurements of the bores. The tools to take these measurements can be quite expensive. If you don't think that refurbishing engines is something you'll be doing often, consider taking the engine and parts to a machine shop. Don't forget your service manual—the shop will need the specs. The shop will take these measurements, evaluate the results, and generally inspect other areas at the same time. If the shop recommends additional work and you have them do it, the evaluation will often be free or at least added to the bill at a reduced rate. Even so, the evaluation charge is still usually quite reasonable—I have seen charges in the $30-$75 range. Although not exactly pocket change, it's much less expensive than purchasing even one of the measurement tools if you did it yourself. If you have these tools, or are willing to purchase them and want to do the work yourself, I'll tell you what to do with it in a moment.

The connecting rods may use two-piece, steel-backed insertable bearings, or the rod may have babbitt-lined

(continued)

PISTONS REMOVAL AND CYLIDER BORE RESTORATION—ALL TRACTORS

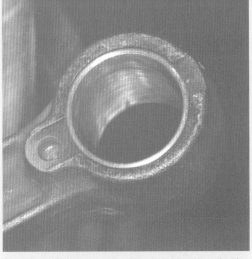

When reconditioning connecting rods, don't forget the wrist-pin bushing. Here, a new bushing has been installed and lightly honed to size for a press fit of the pin.

Shown here are two types of marks you'll find on connecting rods. The rod on the left says, "I belong on journal/bore #1." Two dots on the rod and cap would mean bore #2. It's obvious which bore the other style belongs to. The marks also tell you how to assemble the rods; and they should always line up on the same side.

bearings. If your connecting rods are babbitt lined, and the bearing condition or clearance measurement indicate bearing replacement, you have no choice but to send them out to a shop that does babbitt bearing pouring. This isn't something you'll be able to do yourself. The shop that does this, however, will need to know the crankshaft-rod journal diameter. At this point you won't be able to determine if the crankshaft will have to be machined or replaced, so hold on to your babbitt-lined rod until further work and assessment is done to the crankshaft. You can, however, replace the wrist-pin bushing at this time. If you are replacing the pistons, new wrist pins should be purchased. Once the new pin is in hand, or if you are reusing your old pin, you can ream and hone the bushing to match your wrist pins.

Look at the top of the piston to see any decimal number that may be stamped on the top. This will be a three-digit number, possibly with a leading decimal point. If you find one, this means the pistons were replaced in the past and that the cylinder bore was enlarged and replacement pistons were used. For example, if you find the number .045, this tells you that the bore was expanded by 45 thousandths of an inch, and matching oversized pistons were installed. Considering

PISTONS REMOVAL AND CYLIDER BORE RESTORATION—ALL TRACTORS (CONTINUED)

This is the connecting rod cap of a spun babbitt connecting rod. The babbitt layer is the very thin layer of gray that you see on the inside, underneath the thicker, darker area. It's worn and lightly scored, and clearly in need of babbitt, though many rods are in even worse condition.

After disassembling your engine, you may find problems like this. This piston is burnt, probably from pre-ignition. You can see the erosion along the circumference; this one will have to be replaced. **Gary Uken**

Here are a few examples of the kinds of marks found on the top of pistons. The first one indicates use on a Model 520 LP gas tractor. The second mark indicates it should be used on a Model 630 gas tractor. The marks also indicate the orientation of the piston in the bore. The third shows the wide variety of sizes and styles of pistons used in John Deere tractors. The center and right pistons are the 520 and 630 pistons mentioned above, and are aluminum pistons. The left piston is from a Model B, and is cast iron. Note the raised crown on the 520 piston; a similar raised crown also is found on high-altitude pistons.

the age of these tractors, usually the engine has been rebuilt at least once.

Next, take cylinder-bore diameter measurements. This can be done with a special bore gauge than can be purchased at auto supply stores; instructions are included. Take several measurements of the bore at evenly spaced angles, approximately one-half to one-third of the way down the bore. Record these measurements. Compare the measurements and the variability between the measurements with the specification in the service manual. Keep in mind that if your engine's bore has been enlarged in the past, the diameter measurements will not match the manual's stock standard sizes. If this is the case, remember that the more important specifications such as wear limits and variability specification still apply.

For example, if your service manual states that a 5-inch bore has a wear limit of 5.007 inches, then that 7 thousandths of an inch is the maximum wear that applies to all bore diameters—even if your engine has a pair of 90 thousandths oversized bores. In other words, your 0.090-inch oversized bore must have bore diameters between 5.090 inches and 5.097 inches to be considered "within specifications." If the bores don't hold up to specification, then the engine bores will have to be bored oversize, and

(continued)

Cleaning the ring grooves of your pistons is very important if you are going to reuse the pistons. Shown here is a piston-ring groove-cleaning tool that makes short work of the process.

This photograph shows the oversize stamping in great detail. All oversize pistons are supposed to carry this marking, but some will be illegible. Also, this is the only mark you should trust; not the mark on the box, invoice or packing slip. As soon as you receive new oversize pistons, check the stamp.

Here is an example of oversize piston rings. These rings are designed to be installed on a .045 inch oversize piston, that will be installed in an engine bore that also is .045 inch oversize.

New pistons are usually aluminum. Here is a set of brand-new aluminum M&W pistons for a John Deere Model B.

When refurbishing pistons, new wrist-pin clips should be used. Be absolutely certain the clips sit within the grooves when installing them. It's typical that these clips may be only partially seated, resulting in unpleasant side effects later on.

Installing the piston rings requires a piston ring expander that safely expands the rings without breaking them. Begin expanding the rings farthest away from the end you are sliding them over.

The piston ring on this vertical-engine piston was placed in the top groove for photographic purposes. You should start installing the rings in the third groove from the top since you are sliding the rings down from the top (The fourth, wider groove is for the oil control ring and it can be installed from the bottom). The end gap, which is the gap between the ends of the ring, is clearly visible here. The size of this gap is important; before installation onto the piston, each ring in turn should be slid squarely into a well oiled cylinder bore, and this gap should be measured. Hand grind the ends of the rings with a file to obtain a gap that meets specification. If the gap is too large, then the rings are the wrong size, or style, for your tractor and you need to obtain new ones. When installing the rings onto the piston, be sure to offset the end gaps; the end gaps of the rings on each piston should never line up.

This photograph shows the oversize stamping in great detail. All oversize pistons are supposed to carry this marking, but some will be illegible. Also, this is the only mark you should trust; not the mark on the box, invoice or packing slip. As soon as you receive new oversize pistons, check the stamp.

Here is a photograph of a well-honed cylinder bore. The crosshatches are consistent, are deep enough, and are about 30 degrees out of phase. Practice on scrap engines until your honing skills produce results similar to these.

you will have to purchase a pair of new oversized pistons and matching ring set. Any competent machine shop can perform the boring operation. If the bores are already at the maximum oversize (usually 0.125 inch), then custom sleeves will have to be made to fit inside the bores of the cylinder block. These sleeves are then bored to match the piston sizes. Although this certainly adds some expense, it is usually easier, and not much more expensive, than finding a good, used cylinder block.

Next, inspect the piston-ring and wrist-pin clip grooves for abnormal or asymmetrical wear. Any unusual, noticeable wear of the grooves indicates a piston that must be replaced. Take measurements of the piston. First, measure the diameter of the piston at several places. Take two measurements of the piston skirt thickness (the lower portion of the piston, about one-third of the way up from the bottom, but not directly below the wrist-pin holes) with a micrometer. These measurements are compared against your service manual to determine if

piston wear is advanced enough to warrant replacement. If new pistons are used, the cylinder should be bored even if the bore measurements are within specification. Also, the pistons should be replaced as a complete set, never individually.

Eventually, all this information and these decisions will tell you whether you need to bore or sleeve the

Tips & Tricks

• Always replace pistons as a set—never individually

• Due to the cost and scarcity of replacement camshafts, most restorers ignore cam lobe wear as a reason for replacement as long as the lobe wear is minimal enough to be compensated for by valve-lash adjustments.

• The gasket between the maincase and the cylinder block of horizontal engines is a common source of leaks. Be sure you install this gasket properly and coat both surfaces thoroughly with gasket sealant.

cylinders, replace pistons, and grind the crankshaft. After the decisions are made, any and all machine work is done, and all of your parts are cleaned and ready to go, you need to hone your cylinder bore.

A cylinder bore hone attached to a variable-speed drill will do the job for you. Simply work the hone up and down in the bore, flushing the bore frequently with a kerosene-diesel fuel mixture to cool the stones and remove grit and metal particles. Hone just enough to leave a distinct and complete pattern of scratches in the bore. Match the drill speed and up and down movement so the downward spiral of scratches are about 30 degrees out of phase from the upward spiral of scratches. The coverage of the scratches should be complete, but don't remove too much metal. After cleaning the bores from this operation, double-check fit of the pistons.

Freeing a Stuck Engine

If the tractor you bought has a stuck engine, there are several methods you can use to try to free the engine. First, you'll need to free the block (horizontal-engine tractors) from the tractor, or remove the crankcase from the torque tube and mount the engine to a stand (vertical engines). The stuck pistons and attached connecting rods will still be in tow and the rods will dangle underneath the block. On vertical-engine tractors, you must also ream the ridge from the top of the bore. Set horizontal-engine blocks on a simple wooden stand on the ground. Before beginning, determine if you can save the pistons and rings. If you can't save the pistons, you can crack them out. Simply place the engine block upside down on the ground, and using a heavy mallet and a strong steel bar, break off the top of the piston. Piston-top removal has the effect of narrowing the piston, freeing it and the rings from the sides of the bore. Reverse the cylinder block so you can drive the pistons out from the block (through the bottom for horizontal engine tractors, through the top for vertical engine tractors). Then, using the mallet and a block of wood placed on a wrist-pin boss, beat the piston and rod down and out of the bore.

If you can save the pistons, remove all of the excess rust and crud you can from around the top of the piston. Squirt phosphoric acid around the piston/cylinder bore junction to remove additional rust. Turn the block upside down after 15 minutes to drain and dry the acid. Then apply the four Ps: penetrating fluid, pressure, patience, and prayer. The basic idea is to apply all four in equal quantities every day or two until either you or the pistons give up. This could take overnight, or it could take three months, but eventually you or the pistons will come unhinged and give up. Specifically, start by applying the fluid, waiting a day or two, then pounding on the tops of the pistons with a mallet and a block of wood. If the pistons still don't budge, repeat this process every day or so until they start to move.

If after a few weeks this doesn't do the trick, mount the engine block on a shop press table. Apply liberal doses of penetrating fluid, and then protect the top of the piston by placing a strong steel disc on top of the piston. Apply moderate pressure on the top of the piston with the press and leave the assembly overnight without relieving the pressure on the press. Repeat this every day or two, applying slightly more pressure each day. If after a few days the pistons still won't budge, then they are stuck in a serious way, and their reuse, even if you can get them out of the bores, is questionable. You will have to break them out, as noted above.

CYLINDER-HEAD AND BLOCK RESTORATION

The cylinder head and block—though static chunks of cast iron—need restoration too. They should first be thoroughly cleaned inside and out. If any of these parts go out to a machine shop, they will thoroughly clean them, so you can skip this step if you send the block or head out for work. Ideally, the manifold mating surface on the head (or block of a flathead), the surfaces on both the head and the block where they mate, and the cylinder bores will be refurbished. The intake manifold mating surfaces and the surfaces of the head and block where they mate should be clean, flat, and true. Over time, these castings may change shape in these areas. In these areas if this has happened to either the block or head, these surfaces will also need to be machined flat and true in a process called milling, also commonly referred to as decking. To see if the surfaces need to be milled, lay a mechanic's straight-edge over these surfaces in several orientations. If you can fit a .080-inch feeler gauge through any gap between the straight edge and the surface, you should have both the head and block surfaces milled. For the manifold surface, you should not be able to fit a .125-inch feeler gauge under the straight edge. Any competent machine shop can handle these milling chores for you.

Tips & Tricks
• Honing cylinder bores properly isn't hard, but it does take a little work to become proficient. Practice the skill on scrap engine blocks from the junkyard to gain experience.

Mechanical Restoration

Crankshaft restoration means assessing, possibly machining (a process called grinding), and cleaning the crankshaft to return it to serviceable condition. The first step in assessing the crankshaft is measuring the main-bearing clearance if your tractor has adjustable-type bearings. The later-model horizontal-engine tractors from late letter series onward, use one-piece nonadjustable main bearings that must be replaced as a unit along with the main-bearing housing. The earlier tractors had adjustable bearings, and their bearing clearance is measured using Plastigage. After getting these main-bearing clearances, we will remove and measure the crankshaft. Based on these clearances and/or measurements, we'll either clean the crankshaft, reuse it as is, or have the crankshaft ground to return it to a serviceable condition. Finally, we'll clean the crankshaft thoroughly and cover the journals with special grease designed for use in engine rebuilding. On all tractors, installation is the reverse of removal, but special care needs to be taken during certain steps; I'll outline those as we go along.

HORIZONTAL-ENGINE TRACTORS

Before starting, remove the flywheel, clutch/belt-pulley assembly, and the right-hand brake assembly if you have not done so already. It's handy to have the wheels either removed or adjusted all the way out (wheel and brake removal are covered in the next chapter). Next, remove the reduction gear cover from the right-hand side of the maincase. Removing the cover and the nut of the driven gear shaft will be required on some models before the cover can come off. Next, remove the left-hand bearing-housing cover by removing the flywheel locating screw (if equipped), and then the flywheel spacer. Please note that some spacer/crankshaft combinations require that you mark the crankshaft and spacer with small index marks so the spacer can be reinstalled correctly. If you see no marks, make these marks yourself just in case later cleaning doesn't reveal them. Remove the pipe plugs that cover the adjusting bolts and loosen these bolts. Measure the clearance using plastigage and perform the same operation on the right-hand main bearings.

Disconnect the oil lines from the bearing housings, if you haven't done so already. Remove both bearing housings completely, in their entirety, from the maincase. Then remove the crankshaft of the horizontal Two-Cylinder engine. It will have to be turned and canted as you pull it out on many of these tractors, but the operation is not too

Flywheel removal starts by finding a registration mark on the crankshaft to facilitate the synchronization of the flywheel to the crankshaft during assembly. Here are several photos that show you the different kinds of marks you'll find on both ends of the crankshaft. The first is a Model 60, with a barely visible "V" mark. Next is the mark on a Model H, and the next mark is from the belt pulley side on a Model B. These marks are important and if you can't find them, make your own before removing belt pulleys and flywheels.

difficult. On the larger tractors, the sheer size of the crankshaft requires that someone supports that portion of the crankshaft inside the maincase as you remove it. Once the crankshaft has been removed, look for any obvious sign of damage to the journals or the splines at the ends of the crankshaft. Next, look for any punch marks or stamps made by previous mechanics that may indicate the crankshaft has been ground already. Often the crankshaft will be stamped with this information on one of the flat spots near the rod or main journals. Make a note of these marks.

VERTICAL-ENGINE TRACTORS

On vertical engines, the crankshaft runs in two nonadjustable split-shell bearings held in place by bearing caps. Assuming you have already removed the piston and rod units described earlier, no additional procedures need to be performed before you begin bearing clearance measurements. The bearing clearance can be measured using Plastigage (see sidebar). After clearance measurement, remove the crankshaft completely, and remove the lower bearing shell. Make sure the bearing shells and caps are kept together as a set, and their proper position in the engine block (front or back) is marked on them. Lift out the crankshaft.

Tips & Tricks

• Cracks in the cylinder block and head can usually be seen with a thorough inspection, but some cannot. Machine shops have the equipment, supplies, and tooling to look for and repair hairline or hidden cracks. If you suspect cracks or just want to be sure your casting doesn't have any, find a shop that will perform casting crack checks for you.

CRANKSHAFT MEASUREMENT AND ASSESSMENT

To check the main journals, first visually inspect them. Any gouges or grooves you can catch a fingernail in require grinding. Do likewise with any rust or other significant corrosion. Take measurements of the crankshaft, the main journals (the part of the crankshaft that runs in the main bearings), and the rod journals (that part of the crankshaft that runs in the connecting-rod bearings). All parts should be cleaned before measurement. Measure each journal twice, rotating the caliper 90 degrees between the two measurements. These measurements represent the current diameter of each journal. The difference between the two measurements indicates how "out-of-round" the journals are. The manual for your tractor should tell you what the diameter and the out-of-round difference should be. However, it's been my experience that the out-of-round specification is missing in some of the manuals. In the absence of this specification, assume that the out-of-round measurement should be no more than 1.5 percent of the journal diameter.

If all of your measurements fall within specification, and the crankshaft passes your visual inspection, you can reuse the crankshaft as is. If your crankshaft doesn't meet specification, then it will have to be ground to restore it. Even though your crankshaft may have failed the specification at only one or two of the journals, I recommend grinding the entire crankshaft and using all new main and rod bearings. There is no sense trying to save journals or bearings that are at best marginal if the crankshaft has to make a trip to the machine shop anyway. If your crankshaft journals are within specification, your rod and main journals are adjustable, and the bearings are in good shape, then you can reuse the crankshaft and bearing. Be conservative in your decision making. Replacing bearings and grinding crankshafts is never easier and cheaper than at this point. Skip ahead to the adjusting section now if you are reusing all your crankshaft components.

If your crankshaft needs to be ground, the machine shop that does this work can advise you how much of the journal diameter they have to remove to clean up imperfections. For most engines, replacement main bearings are available in 10 thousandths of an inch increments undersized. The shop may say, for example, "We can clean up the journals by taking a tenth off." That means they can clean up the journals by removing a total of 0.010 inch from the diameters of the journals in question. Before letting the shop start, be sure you can purchase main bearings that will match this new dimension (0.010-inch and 0.020-inch undersized bearings are commonly available for most models). If you can't, advise the shop of the size you can obtain, and see if they recommend grinding to that size. Likewise, if the only bearings you can obtain are a larger undersize than your crankshaft (i.e., the machine shop says they need to take your journals to a 0.020-inch grind and the only bearings you can find are 0.010-inch undersized), the machine shop can build up material on your crankshaft journals—usually through spray welding—then grind it down to the dimension called for by your bearings.

As bearings and crankshaft journals wear, excess clearance is created. Adjusting bearings means adding and removing shims from between the bearing halves to increase or decrease the running clearance. Coming up with the right combinations of shims is a matter of trial and error. Plastigage measurements will have to be taken several times, adding and removing the proper thickness of shims each time until you can create the clearance you need. Make sure the shims used in the main journals rest fully against the crankshaft when you install them, and tighten the adjusting bolts; excess oil will pass through the space left between the shims and the crankshaft.

Ideally, the one-piece bearings used in later model tractors arrive presized; further measuring and resizing of the bearing is not necessary. Occasionally, however, these bearings still need to be sized by a machine shop. To verify the fit of one-piece bearings, coat the bearing and crankshaft main journal with engine assembly grease, slip each bearing and housing over its respective main journal, and rotate the housing. The housing and bearing should slip on with very little resistance and should rotate smoothly without binding or stiffness. If you can't get them on, or if they don't turn smoothly after they are on, have a machine shop size them for your crankshaft. Likewise, if the bearings are loose, then you should exchange them for a larger undersize (e.g., from a 0.010-inch to a 0.020-inch undersized) and have them fitted to your main journals.

ADJUSTING MAIN BEARINGS—ALL TRACTORS WITH ADJUSTABLE BEARINGS

1 Here's a John Deere Model H belt-pulley clutch with the cover removed. It's clearly from a light-duty tractor, but its design and assembly/disassembly procedures are similar to that of larger tractors.

2 To remove the reduction-gear cover of some horizontal-engine tractors, remove the transmission counter-shaft bearing cover and then remove the nut on the end of the shaft. The reduction reduction cover then comes right off.

3 After disassembling the belt pulley and removing the transmission counter-shaft bearing cap nut, removal of the reduction cover is as simple as removing about a dozen bolts. Start on the right and work your way to the left so you can hold up the left side while the crankshaft holds up the right side.

4 The reduction cover is almost off. Notice the extensive use of "gasket making" silicone compounds? Unless you have a special circumstance that requires its use, don't plan on ever using these. Use traditional gaskets and gasket sealants during your restoration.

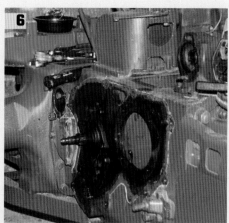

After you remove the reduction cover, remove the reduction gear, shown behind the crankshaft. There is only one nut holding this on, and its removal is straightforward.

This is what the tractor looks like after removal of the right side crankshaft bearing housing and the crankshaft. You now have full access to all of the areas of the main case for additional work and cleaning.

Main bearing work starts by removing the main-bearing housing cover. The photographs feature a John Deere B, but these procedures are fairly representative of all horizontal-engine tractors.

The flywheel spacer comes off next. Notice the notch that registers it to the flywheel. Also, look for an indexing screw in the crankshaft that you need to remove, as shown in some of these photographs.

To get the flywheel spacer moving, you'll have to be a little creative. The instinct is to use the notch in the spacer as a landing for a blunt punch. Only do this as a last resort because this notch has a very specific size and you may enlarge it if you hammer on it too much. Also, tapping the side of the spacer with a hammer will break the thin metal where an oil groove is. Tap on the end of the crankshaft (first protect the end of the crankshaft) with a hammer to loosen the spacer then resort to very light taps made to a blunt steel rod placed in the notch of the spacer. These steps will usually get the spacer moving. This spacer, while not delicate, can still be easily damaged. Take your time and try a couple of different approaches.

The flywheel spacer contains the crankshaft oil seal, shown here as the dark circular band on the inside of the spacer. This should be replaced.

These photographs show two important components of the flywheel/crankshaft engineering. First is the spacer, which serves as a thrust washer and as a spacer to keep the flywheel away from the main-bearing housing. The second photo shows the crankshaft indexing screw. This screw registers the flywheel to the crankshaft and should be removed to prevent damage during crankshaft restoration.

To gain access to the adjusting bolts, remove the pipe plugs.

To remove the main bearing adjusting bolts, remove the nuts after pulling out the cotter pins.

With the pipe plug and the nuts removed, you can pull out the adjusting bolts (shown here).

Remove the interior half of the bearing housing. There is not much clearance between it and the housing; pull it out straight and true.

These photographs show that removing the main bearing housings is pretty straightforward. After verifying that you have loosened and removed the oil lines found inside the crankcase (17), loosen and remove the mounting bolts. The housing is free and can then be pulled off. Be careful not to ding or mar the main bearing still in the housing.

The right side main-bearing housing is simpler, with no spacers or seals to remove. Again, start by removing the adjusting bolts.

Here, the right-side main-bearing housing is being removed. Again, after removing just a few bolts (and after disconnecting the bearing oil line) the housing comes right off.

In this picture, the bolts are off and the housing can be pulled. Note that the free inner-bearing shell is removed before the bearing housing itself is loosened and removed.

After the bearing housings are removed, remove the crankshaft through the right side of the engine. On larger tractors, this requires two people. You'll have to twist and snake it a bit to get it out.

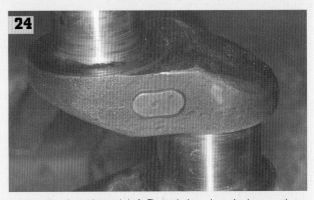

Locate any marks on the crankshaft. The mark shown here simply means that the rod journal beside it is for the connecting rod and piston that occupies bore #2. Other marks may exist that were left behind by a machinist to signify that the crankshaft has been ground. After removal, check the crankshaft over well for any marks or punches.

Mechanical Restoration

Your belt-pulley-mounted clutch is very likely to need significant work to restore it to like-new operation. For safety's sake, you should be very thorough about restoring this, making sure to have all components repaired or restored as necessary. The clutch linkage should be removed at this point if it hasn't been already. Inspect the linkage for any broken parts, or parts that have been badly repaired, and replace them. The three biggest problems of belt-pulley clutches are worn drive disc splines and/or crankshaft splines (in early tractors, the design was improved later), worn clutch facings, and worn clutch-linkage components. The belt-pulley bearing and bushings are covered in the transmission chapter.

Start with a complete disassembly of the clutch. As it is disassembled, every component should be hand-operated in place, and any sign of looseness should be investigated. Check the drive disc and the adjusting disc for any signs of warpage, glazing, or cracking. If the looseness of the drive disk is very minor and the wear of the crankshaft splines is even and symmetrical, then an undersized drive disc (a drive disc with a hub and splines with a slightly smaller diameter) can be used, but otherwise the crankshaft splines should be rebuilt and a new drive disc installed.

The linings of the free-facing discs and the lined disc (some clutches only have free-facing discs) should

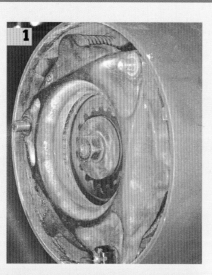

Clutch and belt pulley removal starts with the removal of the clutch-adjusting nuts from the operating bolts. In this photograph, two of these nuts have been removed and one has yet to be removed. Clutch and belt pulley removal starts with the removal of the clutch-adjusting nuts from the operating bolts. In this photograph, two of these nuts have been removed and one has yet to be removed.

You can then remove the clutch-adjusting disc.

After removing the adjusting disc, remove any discs found in front of the drive disc. These should all come off without force. The free disc behind the clutch-adjusting disc has been removed, exposing the sliding-drive disc. This will come off by hand to expose the lined disc, which then can be taken off by hand to expose the drive disc.

Be sure to note any registration marks, and be sure they exist. You'll need these marks when you reinstall the clutch drive disc. Marks vary from model to model, and may not even be visible depending on the condition of the end of the crankshaft, and other factors. Make your own marks if necessary. These marks are from a later Model B.

be inspected. Unless these linings look nearly new, they should be replaced or relined. The operating bolts and clutch dogs and pins should be replaced if any of the parts show wear, especially the operating bolts. These components should operate smoothly and without discernible looseness if your clutch is to operate smoothly. Next, inspect the clutch linkage components for wear and damage. Extensive wear can usually be found on the fork shaft. Likewise, extensive wear is usually found at the clutch-lever pivot bore and pin and the clevis rod pin (and sometimes the clevis bore). Finally, the pulley brake pad should be replaced. Most of this can be repaired through parts replacement or various brazing, welding, and machining operations. Mike Williams, mentioned

in the appendices, does all of the work mentioned here, including the pulley brake pad replacement, necessary for clutch repair. Investing in his work is a wise decision.

Tips & Tricks

• When assembling the clutch, be absolutely sure the drive disc and crankshaft registration marks line up. Otherwise, your engine will develop a noticeable, and sometimes significant, vibration problem.

• Use an antiseizing compound on the clutch operating bolts and dog pivot pins to keep these components operating smoothly for a long time.

Use a standard puller to remove the drive disc. Leave the cap screw in the crankshaft so your puller won't damage the end of the crankshaft. Place the puller's center bolt on the cap bolt and thread the pulling bolts into the holes in the drive disc made for this purpose.

Use the puller to pull the drive disc of the belt pulley gear.

This is the drive disc from a Model B. The splines are only mildly worn and look better than most—if you look closely you'll notice a bit of depression wear has started at the base of the splines. This slight wear, and similar wear on the crankshaft splines, combine to create a noticeable, if not significant, looseness to the drive disc. The friction surfaces are in good shape, though. Often, you see deep striations and gouges that require replacement of the disc.

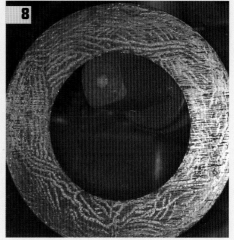

The free-facing disc should be replaced as part of any clutch restoration.

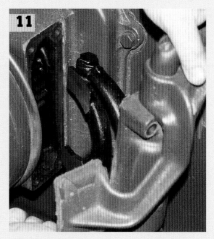

This is the friction surface of the belt pulley. This is in great shape; no rust, gouges, grooves or other defects. If such defects were present, the surface would have to be milled to remove them. The machine shop can't cut too much off this surface or the clutch will not adjust properly, especially if it has been milled before.

Removing the clutch fork bearing, which looks more like a cover than anything else, requires removing only a few bolts. Disconnect the clutch lever first—you can see that the clutch lever has been disconnected here.

Pull the fork bearing and its entire assembly straight out.

At this point, the belt pulley can be removed. You can see the large oil slinger—the part with the spiraled groove. Set the pulley aside for the time being.

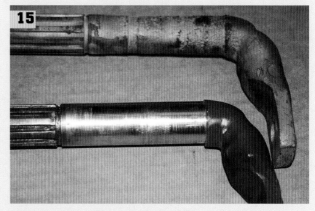

Disassembly of the fork-bearing assembly begins with the removal of a stubborn little lock ring found near the top of the fork shaft.

Here are two fork shafts. Your fork shaft probably looks like the top one; the bottom is how it should look. Restoration of these components is critical if you want a safe, reliable, smoothly operating clutch. Mike Williams did the machining for this fork shaft.

Mechanical Restoration

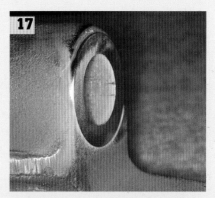

These photographs compare two fork-bearing shaft bores. The bearing on the right shows signs of bore wear. The bearing on the left was restored by bushing the bore with a cast-iron bushing. These bores were not originally bushed; bushing them is the only way to eliminate wear and the sloppy movement of the clutch linkage that wear allows.

Here's a close-up of the cast-iron bushing. The brake fork shaft needs to be built up and repaired with bronze and the proper material to bush the fork bearing bores when using bronze on the shaft is cast iron.

Place a new brake pad on your pulley brake, especially if your pad looks like the one on the right. The pads are easily riveted on. Finally, inspect the brake bore and shank/arm for any signs of bending or cracking.

(Right) Replacing the belt-pulley cover clips is easy with an air-driven peen hammer. The rest of the tools needed are an anvil to shape the backside of the rivet and a method; in this case, C clamps were used to hold the anvil in place.
Gary Uken

These photographs show the setup necessary to rivet the belt-pulley cover clips in place. The new clip is positioned in place, the rivet is placed in the hole, and then it is backed by the anvil and clamped in place. Gary Uken

CLUTCH—BELT-PULLEY-MOUNTED (CONTINUED)

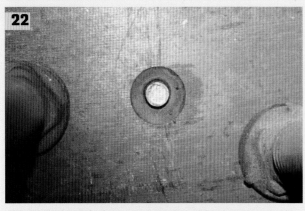

22

The next step is to peen the rivet. Here the rivet, anvil and the clamps are in place. Attach a peening hammer to the air chisel to peen down the rivet into a funnel-shaped head. Gary Uken

23

Here is the final result of the peening operation. The head is symmetrical, without any thin spots or evidence of over-peening. As soon as the head is formed and drawn up against the pulley, you are done; additional blows from the air chisel will only weaken the rivet. Gary Uken

24 **25** **26**

These photographs show the final result. The clips are installed and the holes on the outside circumference can be filled for aesthetic reasons in preparation for paint, or left as-is. Gary Uken

When repairing the clutch of vertical-engine tractors, be sure to replace the clutch thrust bearing, as shown here. Reusing it makes little sense because it is not that expensive, and it's easier to replace it at this point, instead of later on down the road.

CLUTCH—FLYWHEEL-MOUNTED

Flywheel-mounted clutches are simple affairs that are very similar to automotive clutches. Therefore, most local auto parts stores that accept automotive clutches for repair or exchange can handle your John Deere flywheel-mounted clutch. There is little you can do yourself that would be worth the time and effort considering the convenience and reasonable cost of these professional shops. The next step is to surface the flywheel. Any time a clutch disc is relined or replaced, the friction surface of the flywheel should be milled flat and true to remove any ridges or marks created by the old clutch disc. Note that balancing the flywheel and clutch combination is a good idea.

Balancing is something many automotive machine shops can do for you. The shop that will be milling the flywheel friction surface can also balance the flywheel and clutch. Be sure to have them balance these components after you have received the new clutch.

Tips & Tricks

• Some machine shops can balance flywheels as large as those found on John Deere tractors. Although certainly not necessary, balancing the flywheel adds a nice touch to the restoration and minimizes engine vibration.

| TRACTOR OR ENGINE | | VALVE GUIDES | | | | VALVES | | | | | | SPRINGS | |
| MODEL | SERIAL # | I.D. of Valve Guide | | Length of Valve Guide (B, 30-10-25) | Distance of Valve Guide From Head (C, 30-20-25) | Diameter of Valve Stem (D, 30-10-25) | Angle of Valve (E, 30-10-25) | Angle of Seat (F, 30-10-25) | Width of Valve Head (C, 30-10-25) | | Width of Valve Seat (H, 30-10-25) | Compress to | Pounds Pressure |
		Original	Ream to (A, Fig. 30-10-25)						Intake	Exhaust			
A	410000 - 487999	.4375 - .4485	.4385 - .4400	$4^{13}/_{16}$	$1^{3}/_{16}$	Intake: .4335 - .4345 Exhaust: .4375 - .4385	45°	45°	$2^{1}/_{8}$″	$1^{7}/_{8}$″	$3/_{8}$″	$2^{3}/_{4}$″	36 - 44
A	488000 and up	.5000 - .5010	.5010 - .5025	$4^{3}/_{4}$″	$2^{1}/_{8}$″	.4960 - .4970	Intake: 30° Exhaust: 45°	Intake: 30° Exhaust: 45°	$2^{1}/_{4}$″	$2^{1}/_{16}$″	$1/_{8}$″	$2^{3}/_{4}$″	36 - 44
AR-AO-AI	250000 and up	.4375 - .4385	.4385 - .4400	$4^{13}/_{16}$	$1^{5}/_{16}$″	Intake: .4335 - .4345 Exhaust: .4375 - .4385	45°	45°	$2^{1}/_{8}$″	$1^{3}/_{8}$″	$3/_{8}$″	$2^{1}/_{4}$″	36 - 44
AR-AO	260000 and up	.5000 - .5010	.5010 - .5025	$4^{3}/_{4}$″	$2^{1}/_{8}$″	.4960 - .4970	Intake: 30° Exhaust: 45°	Intake: 30° Exhaust: 45°	$2^{3}/_{4}$″	$2^{1}/_{16}$″	$1/_{8}$″	$2^{1}/_{4}$″	36 - 44
B	B1000- B59999	.3750 - .3760	.3760 - .3775	$3^{3}/_{8}$″	$1^{1}/_{8}$″	.3715 - .3725	45°	45°	$1^{3}/_{4}$″	$1^{3}/_{8}$″	$3/_{8}$″	$2^{13}/_{16}$″	28 - 34
B	B60000- B55999	.3750 - .3760	.3760 - .3775	$3^{3}/_{8}$″	$1^{3}/_{16}$″	.3715 - .3725	45°	45°	$1^{3}/_{4}$″	$1^{3}/_{8}$″	$3/_{8}$″	$2^{13}/_{16}$″	28 - 34
B	B96000 and up	.4375 - .4385	.4385 - .4400	$3^{3}/_{8}$″	Intake: $1^{11}/_{16}$″ Exhaust: $1^{11}/_{16}$″	.4335 - .4345	Intake: 30° Exhaust: 45°	Intake: 30° Exhaust: 45°	$1^{13}/_{16}$″	$1^{13}/_{16}$″	$1/_{8}$″	$2^{13}/_{16}$″	35 - 39
BR-BO-BI	B325000 and up	.3750 - .3760	.3760 - .3775	$3^{7}/_{8}$″	$1^{1}/_{16}$″	.3715 - .3725	45°	45°	$1^{3}/_{4}$″	$1^{5}/_{8}$″	$1/_{8}$″	$2^{13}/_{16}$″	28 - 34
G	G1000- G12999	.5625 - .5635	.5635 - .5650	Intake: $4^{11}/_{16}$″ Exhaust: $4^{11}/_{16}$″	$1^{11}/_{16}$″	.5575 - .5595	45°	45°	$2^{9}/_{16}$″	$2^{7}/_{16}$″	$11/_{16}$″	$3^{3}/_{8}$″	56 - 58
G GM	G13000 and up	.5625 - .5635	.5635 - .5650	$5^{3}/_{4}$″	$2^{1}/_{4}$″	.5575 - .5595	Intake: 30° Exhaust: 45°	Intake: 30° Exhaust: 45°	$2^{5}/_{8}$″	$2^{7}/_{8}$″	$11/_{16}$″	$3^{3}/_{8}$″	56 - 58
D	30400 100943	.6250 - .6260	.6260 - .6280	4″	$1^{3}/_{4}$″	.6220 - .6230	30°	30°	$2^{13}/_{16}$″	$2^{11}/_{16}$″	$5/_{16}$″	3″	60 - 75
D	100944 and up	.6250 - .6260	.6260 - .6280	$5^{1}/_{16}$″	$1^{5}/_{8}$″	.6200 - .6220	30°	30°	$2^{3}/_{4}$″	$2^{3}/_{4}$″	$5/_{16}$″	$3^{3}/_{8}$″	58 - 72
H	H1000 and up	.3750 - .3760	.3760 - .3775	$3^{1}/_{8}$″	$1^{11}/_{16}$″	.3715 - .3725	Intake: 30° Exhaust: 45°	Intake: 30° Exhaust: 45°	$1^{13}/_{16}$″	$1^{9}/_{16}$″	$1/_{8}$″	$2^{5}/_{8}$″	62 - 68
GP-O-WT	A11	.5000 - .5010	Intake: .5020 - .5050 Exhaust: .5010 - .5030	$4^{13}/_{16}$	*$7/_{16}$″	.4960 - .4970	45°	45°	$2^{3}/_{16}$″	$2^{9}/_{16}$″	$3/_{16}$″	†$2^{7}/_{8}$″	†48 - 58
L	625000- 639000	.3120 - .3130	.3120 - .3130	- - - -	#$15/_{16}$″	.3095 - .3105	30°	30°	$1^{1}/_{4}$″	$1^{1}/_{8}$″	$1/_{8}$″	$1^{1}/_{8}$″	45 - 53
L	640000 and up	.3120 - .3130	.3120 - .3130	- - - -	#$3/_{4}$″	.3095 - .3105	30°	30°	$1^{1}/_{4}$″	$1^{1}/_{8}$″	$1/_{8}$″	$1^{1}/_{8}$″	45 - 53
LI-LA-LU- LUC-LUS- PV	A11	.3120 - .3130	.3120 - .3130	- - - -	#$3/_{4}$″	.3095 - .3105	30°	30°	$1^{1}/_{4}$″	$1^{1}/_{8}$″	$1/_{8}$″	$1^{1}/_{8}$″	45 - 53
M Series	M10000 and up MC10000 and up MT10000 and up	.3695 - .3670	.3745 - .3760	- - - -	$2^{3}/_{16}$″	.3715 - .3725	Intake: 30° Exhaust: 45°	Intake: 30° Exhaust: 45°	$1^{13}/_{16}$″	$1^{9}/_{16}$″	Intake: $1/_{8}$″ Exhaust: $3/_{16}$″	2″	52

* Dimension from face of cylinder to rear of guide
† GP200111 - GP229835: 3″ —- 50-65 lbs.
# Dimension from top of block to top of valve guide

Tips & Tricks

• Make sure the oil slinger of the clutch is clean, and all oil grooves are free of dirt, grease, and grime.

• The "lip side" of a head gasket (the side where you can see the overlap of the metal edging) is installed so it faces the cylinder head.

• Always tighten cylinder-head bolts or nuts in two stages using a torque wrench to verify they are being tightened properly. First tighten the nuts or bolts to 60 percent of final torque values. Then tighten them to the final torque values. Be sure to follow the tightening pattern outlined in your manual.

• When installing gaskets, always use gasket material of similar composition and thickness as the originals. Under no circumstances should you use the modern silicon-based gasket-making compounds commonly referred to as "gasket goo," with one exception: The water manifold cylinder head mating surface is usually warped and inconsistent. If you do not have these surfaces milled flat and true, you may have problems with coolant leakage. In this case, you may have no option but to use a gasket-making compound.

Mechanical Restoration

Valvetrain restoration involves the restoration of the valves, the valve guides and springs, rocker arms, cam followers or tappets, and the camshaft assembly. Beginning the operation requires making an inspection of the valves where the face of the valve is seated against the cylinder head or block. There are three things to check for: the amount of valve stem and valve guide bore wear, the general condition of the entire valve (e.g., straight stem, no corrosion on the stem), and acceptable valve face, seat, and "margin" dimensions. The accompanying diagram will help you identify the margin and face. The last thing you need to inspect is the valve seat. This is the area on the cylinder head or block that the valve face mates to. Likewise, this area should show no pitting or corrosion.

Depending on the number of hours on your tractor's engine and how recently any previous rebuild was performed, the valves and seats might be in good enough condition to reuse as they are. Valve performance is so critical to overall engine operation that restoring or replacing your current valves, springs, and guides should be standard procedure, unless they clearly are in excellent shape. As I have said many times in this book, replacing and restoring parts and systems will never be any cheaper or easier than now. If you are unsure, take your valve assembly to a machine shop, including the cylinder head or block, so they can examine the seats. They can give you a better recommendation for your particular circumstance. If you do reuse your valves, be sure to return each component to the location it came from.

To check these three valve condition parameters, perform the following procedures. First, measure the valve margin and compare these values to those in your manual. To check the condition of the seat and face, buff them clean and look for any pitting or rust. If the pits or rust can be felt when the valve or seat is rubbed with your finger, then the seats should be cut and the valve faces reground by a

machine shop. To check stem and bore wear, measure each at three points along their length and compare them to the specifications in your manual. If the diameter is acceptable compared to the specifications, then simply replace the valve guides. New replacement guides are already reamed to match valve stems that are within factory-wear specification and require no further reaming. Keep in mind that some NOS valve guides will require that you ream the guides to match the valve stem diameters. Though reaming guides is not horribly difficult, it is yet another set of skills and tools you'll need to acquire. The machine shop that is doing your other engine work can take care of this for you easily.

The next step is to check the tension of your valve springs. The tension specification is the amount of weight required to compress the spring a certain distance. Your service manual will specify both the weight and the distances. The specification is usually expressed twice in the manual, once as a "valve-closed length" (the length of the spring when the valve is closed), and a "valve-open length" (the length of the valve spring when the valve is open). Also expressed with these two lengths is the weight required to compress the spring to the valve-open position. Valve spring testers can often be rented, but a little ingenuity, accurate scales, and a carpenter's adjustable T-square can suffice for your own homegrown tension readings.

If you have a John Deere B, you should inspect the pushrod tubes (also known as sleeves). These are the tubes that pass from the bottom of the cylinder head, through its coolant cavity, up to the top of the cylinder head. Look for signs of coolant leaks or damage. The pushrod tubes can be replaced by pressing or pulling them through the top (valvetrain side) of the cylinder head.

Next, the system that operates the valves needs to be restored. The camshaft has to be removed to do this, but there are a few items you'll need to remove if you haven't done so already. On horizontal-engine tractors, the oil pump must be removed. On vertical Two-Cylinder tractors, both the oil pump and the ignition distributor or magneto have to be removed. After these are removed, take the time to make a mark that will "register" the camshaft gear to the crankshaft gear. Although marks were provided at the factory, they are often illegible. The marks are made with a center punch. Simply make a mark on the side of a camshaft tooth, then make a mark on the side of the crankshaft timing gear just below the "valley" (the space between two teeth) that the marked camshaft geartooth mates into. This will help you install the camshaft correctly

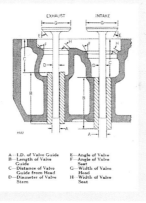

This drawing and chart will guide you or your machinist in rebuilding and machining the valves and related parts. The letters all refer to critical valve and seat measurements. Using the chart, look up the letter corresponding to the measurement you need, then cross reference it to your model of tractor. The measurement found at the intersection will give you the factory specification for the measurement. (Charts and diagram courtesy of Deere & Company)

when assembling the engine. From here, the procedures differ between the two different kinds of engines.

On vertical Two-Cylinder engines with a camshaft-driven hydraulic pump (M, 30, 40, and their kin) you must remove the hydraulic pump first. The hydraulic lines should have been removed during initial disassembly, so the pump can easily be removed by unbolting it from the timing gear cover. Next, remove the front timing-gear cover of the engine. This will give you access to the camshaft. It is removed by unbolting the camshaft's thrust plate (behind the camshaft gear) from the cylinder block. Hold the camshaft followers (the mushroom-shaped parts that ride the camshaft lobes and raise and lower the pushrods) up away from the camshaft as you carefully withdraw the camshaft from the engine. The cam followers will drop out of the block as the camshaft clears each follower, so be sure to catch them.

On horizontal Two-Cylinder engines, several assemblies will have to be removed first to gain access to the camshaft. To start, remove the governor housing from the top of the maincase. Depending on the model, there may be one or more oil lines connected to the governor

housing, so remove them first. Then remove the distributor or magneto. The oil-pump drive disengagement was discussed a little earlier; if you haven't yet removed it, do so now. Unbolt the bearing cover that the fan shaft protrudes from. The fan shaft will pull out. Then unbolt the governor housing from the maincase; one of the bolts may be different than the others, depending on the model. If so, its location should be noted so it can be returned to the same spot during assembly later on.

Start camshaft removal by working inside the crankcase; making a registration mark between the camshaft gear and camshaft. Next, remove all oil lines from the maincase. The left-side camshaft bearing housing is removed by unbolting it from the maincase. Then remove the bracket that houses the cam followers that is bolted to the top of the maincase. The gear that drives the oil pump will fall at this point, so be sure to catch it. Remove the right hand side camshaft bearing cover. Then remove the camshaft gear from the camshaft. Push the camshaft out through the right-hand side of the maincase. Reach into the maincase and pull out the camshaft gear; inspect the camshaft and camshaft gear for abnormal wear or damage.

CAMSHAFT RESTORATION AND INSTALLATION—VERTICAL-ENGINE TRACTORS

Once the camshaft is removed, the camshaft and camshaft timing gear should be inspected for damage. Replace any component that shows damage. Next, the camshaft journals (the round barrel parts of the camshaft that ride in the bearings) should be measured. Then, using inside micrometers, measure the inside diameter of the camshaft bearings. Use the service manual to compare measure-

ments. If either or both measurements indicate wear that is beyond specification, then the journals should be reground to a smaller standard size, and new replacement oversized bearings purchased. A machine shop should press and ream the bearings for you. The thrust plate controls camshaft endplay (its side-to-side movement); therefore, there is no procedure to adjust the endplay.

CAMSHAFT RESTORATION AND INSTALLATION—HORIZONTAL-ENGINE TRACTORS

If you are going to restore the crankshaft, do that next. The camshaft should be installed after the crankshaft is restored and installed. Camshaft bearings vary considerably among models and even within serial number ranges within the same model. Models A and G use roller bearings, while the H uses ball bearings; the B and D use bushed housings. In all cases, the bearings should be evaluated and replaced as part of a restoration. Inspect all other removed components of the valvetrain for abnormal damage and wear, such as the camshaft followers and their bracket, pushrods, and oil-pump drive gear. When reinstalling these components, realize that the model H controls the timing-gear lash (how closely the camshaft gear and crankshaft gear mesh) through the

use of an eccentric bearing housing. The bearing housing should be installed with this in mind. If the gear lash is incorrect when you reassemble, you can rotate the housing 90 degrees either clockwise or counterclockwise to arrive at a lash that is appropriate. Timing-gear lash is not adjustable on most other models.

The camshaft endplay is controlled on some models through the use of gaskets on the bearing housing(s). On the remainder of the models, endplay is controlled with a spring in the right-side bearing housing. Check camshaft endplay when reinstalling, being sure to use a gasket thickness that allows you to arrive at a specification measurement. Visually inspect the spring to verify its soundness and that it is acceptable for further use.

Mechanical Restoration

Disassemble the oil pump and completely clean the assembly. Reassemble using an oil-pump refurbishment kit available through most part suppliers. This typically includes a new set of gears, gaskets, and possibly a shaft or two depending on the make of the oil-pump refurbishment kit. Coat all parts with clean 30-weight oil as you assemble it. Reinstall the oil pump and lines, in the reverse of the procedures you used to take it apart.

Visually inspect the governor and manually operate it, looking for any abnormal movements, excessive looseness, or damage. If all seems to be in order, you can reinstall it. If not, disassemble the governor and replace all gaskets and bearings, including the thrust bearings. If you disassemble the governor from horizontal-engine John Deere tractors, be aware that the governor assembly uses gaskets to adjust the lash between the two pinion gears found inside. The gear lash of the governor drive-pinion gear and the fan-shaft pinion is adjusted by the thickness of the gaskets found under the left-hand cover and the fan-shaft bearing cover. Gaskets are available from most parts suppliers, but in this case I make my own out of very thin gasket materials, and then stack multiple gaskets until the lash is correct. When is the lash correct? Because there are no specifications in some manuals, you'll have to do this by feel. Pinion gears that are mated correctly never leave an assembly that feels loose. Likewise, the lash is never so tight as to leave an assembly feeling rough or tight when turned by hand. It is better to err slightly to

This is the bevel pinion gear that drives the fan shaft and is driven by the governor bevel pinion gear. This gear is in good shape and shows very little wear. Tractors that have seen quite a few hours will show a lot of wear; inspect these closely.

the side of looseness to prevent gear damage, but excessive wear will occur if it is too loose.

To install the governor on vertical Two-Cylinder engines, simply couple the housing to the block and tighten it. The process is more involved for horizontal engines because the governor case also drives the magneto, requiring both the governor and the magneto to be synchronized with the crankshaft. To do this, turn the crankshaft so the timing mark on the camshaft is visible and at the top of the camshaft timing gear. Turn the governor drive shaft until the timing mark is visible below the governor body. Install the governor body on the tractor by matching the timing marks on the camshaft timing gear with the governor drive gear. If the timing marks are not visible, then turn the flywheel until the "LH Impulse" timing mark found on the flywheel aligns with the gear case mark. At this time, turn the governor shaft until the magneto or distributor-drive coupling is perfectly horizontal. Hook up any oil lines as needed, then fasten the governor to the maincase.

Using Plastigage

The most important measurements you will take during an engine rebuild are that of the rod and main-bearing running clearance. This is the measurement of the space between the crankshaft journals and the journal bearings. If there is too much clearance, then oil pressure within the engine will be hard to maintain and the bearings will wear at an accelerated rate. Too little clearance and the bearings may overheat and fail or spin within their housings, causing expensive damage to the bearing housings. Your main goal during a lower engine rebuild is to create proper rod and main-bearing running clearances.

Measure this clearance with a product called Plastigage. This product consists of soft plastic "threads" that give accurate clearance readings. It gives these readings by crushing in a predictable, accurate way, allowing you to measure the amount of crush with a special rule included with the

Plastigage product. This rule interpolates the running clearance by the amount of crush.

To use the product, make sure the crankshaft journals and bearings are clean. Place the Plastigage thread parallel to the longitudinal axis, directly on the crankshaft journal that you are measuring. Then install the bearing cap (with the bearing installed), and tighten the cap to the specifications listed in your service manual. Be careful not to turn the crankshaft while the bearing cap is installed and the Plastigage thread is in place. Remove the bearing cap. The Plastigage thread will remain on the journal, and will be flattened. Using the rule provided, compare the width of the crushed Plastigage with the width markings on the rule. The rule will translate the width to an actual clearance measurement. Make sure to remove the Plastigage and clean the bearing and journal surfaces for final assembly.

Finish up the interior portion of the engine restoration by installing any remaining oil lines and verifying the soundness of all connections and the tightness of all fasteners. Now is the time to double- and triple-check everything because at this point you are ready to close up the engine. Make sure mechanical nut- and bolt-locking wires and pins are in place and secure, freeze plugs and oil galley plugs are installed, and that all fasteners with a torque specificaton, such as the cylinder-head studs or bolts, have been tightened to proper torque values. With the core parts of the engine restored, you are well on your way to finishing the mechanical restoration. There are a few more areas that require attention, and those are the systems responsible for fuel and ignition delivery, cooling, and engine governing. In the next chapter I'll discuss those systems, and explain how to test the engine.

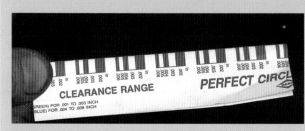

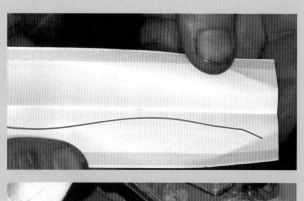

Plastigage comes in long, thin packages and is available in three colors, each covering a different clearance range. Red is for .002 inch-.006 inch, which is the clearance range for John Deere main bearings. The photograph to the right shows the Plastigage thread; just a small piece is needed for each test.

Place the Plastigage on the main journal of the crankshaft, then install the bearing cap making sure to torque the adjusting bolts to factory specification. Remove the cap again; the Plastigage should look like this.

After removing the inner half of the main bearing housing, place a piece of Plastigage on the main bearing journal. Hold it in place with a drop of oil, and replace the inner half of the bearing housing. Install the adjusting bolts and torque them to factory specifications.

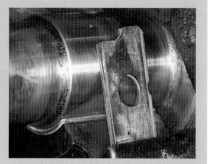

After removing the inner bearing cap again, this is what you will find: The Plastigage is compressed in direct relation to the amount of clearance between the bearing and crankshaft.

Read your Plastigage measurement. Here is a main-bearing running clearance of approximately .0035 inch. The clearance was originally larger, but the removal of a shim put it within factory specification of .002 inch-.006 inch.

If your running clearance is not correct, but the crankshaft and bearings are serviceable, you can add and remove shims from the shim packs, as shown, to create the proper running clearance.

Engine Systems Restoration and Testing

"All parts should go together without forcing. You must remember
that the parts you are reassembling were disassembled by you. Therefore,
if you can't get them together again, there must be a reason.
By all means, do not use a hammer."
—IBM maintenance manual, 1925

A John Deere Two-Cylinder engine restoration is only as good as the restoration of the fuel and ignition delivery systems. A weak magneto or gummed-up carburetor attached to a brand-new engine will leave you with an engine that performs as badly, if it runs at all, as the day you brought it into the shop for restoration. Under no circumstances should you skip a full and complete restoration of these systems during the tractor's restoration. Although the restoration procedures for these components can be mastered by those willing to learn, these systems are usually difficult to restore properly without more than a beginner's level of experience and understanding of engines.

Professional shops have the correct parts and a greater understanding of these systems. Unlike most engine systems, these systems are the most likely to require specialized tools to service and test afterward, requiring a large investment in equipment and tools. I recommend engine systems such as the ignition delivery (magneto, distributor), fuel delivery (carburetors and diesel fuel injection), water pumps, power-steering system, starters, and generators be restored professionally. There are many companies specializing in these services listed in the appendices of this book. I've either visited or sent work to most of them, and recommend them.

Included in this chapter are a number of photographs that will guide you, step by step, through the process of carburetor, magneto, and distributor restoration. I have also included a few photos of a diesel fuel pump and injection system to aid those who want to understand them better. For more information, I suggest you pick up a copy of the John Deere Service Publication titled, *Tractors and Engines (General)*, publication #SM-200; it's available from Deere or any well-stocked manual dealer. Contact information for manuals and sources can be found in the appendices.

Another source of information, as I mentioned earlier, is my book *How to Restore Your Farm Tractor Engine*. It covers in more detail magnetos, carburetors, and distributors. Also, MBI Publishing Company publishes a book on tractor magnetos titled *How to Restore Your Tractor Magneto* by Neil Yerigan; this also will prove indispensable.

Even if you don't want to restore these systems yourself, most of you would enjoy knowing how these shops restore the parts and components. Plus, this section will show problem areas that may exist on your tractor—information that will help you make educated decisions regarding which parts and components need replacement, repair, or simply restoration.

Tips & Tricks

When testing your engine, triple-check the following items before starting:

- Double-check the mounting of flywheels on all types of engines. This is especially critical for horizontal engines.
- Verify that head bolts have been tightened to proper torque values.
- Be sure that fuel does not leak from your newly restored carburetor.
- Use a clean and restored gas tank, or a safe temporary tank, to feed the newly restored carburetor.
- Before initial starting, spin the engine using the starter or another tractor to verify that the engine will build oil pressure. You should also prime the oil delivery system by pumping oil into one of the oil ports in the head or external gauge or line (all tractors), or an oil line found under the governor (horizontal-engine tractors).

Starters and generators should be restored professionally. Typically, they will be returned to you in like-new condition with complete paint job done to your specification. Don't forget to replace the solenoid and voltage regulator.

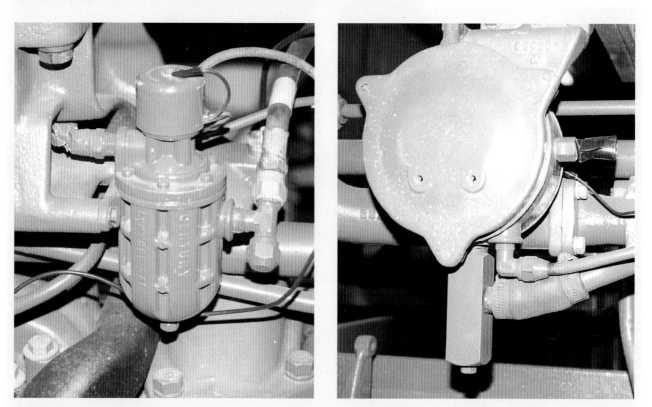

These photographs illustrate two devices specific to a tractor that uses LP fuel. The first photograph shows the strainer and cut-off, and the second photograph shows the expansion chamber.

Tips & Tricks

• Testing Safety Tip: Because carburetors sit above the cylinders in John Deere Two-Cylinder, horizontal-engine tractors, fuel leaking past the needle valve in the carburetor over time will dump raw gas into one or more cylinders. Also, checking for spark at the spark plug by removing the spark plug, hooking it back up to the plug wire, and then grounding it on the engine block is a terrible accident waiting to happen. If these two conditions exist, as soon as you spin the engine, raw gas will be pushed out of the spark plug hole during the compression stroke just as the magneto lights the plug and unfortunately, the raw gas too. I have heard of many cases of this happening and have verified two of them. Fortunately neither resulted in death, but caused severe burns and a hospital stay. The resulting fire destroyed the tractors and the shops these folks were in. In neither case did they suspect the carburetor was leaking. Never check for a spark until you are certain the cylinder is free of excessive fuel, and always ground the plug away from the spark plug hole.

RESTORING A CARBURETOR

Keeping a carburetor running is a little like plumbing: Keep all of the passageways clean and you'll never have a problem. The carburetor has numerous passageways that are difficult to access. The size of the passageways and the smoothness of their walls is critically important. To top that off, you have to make sure lots of air gets in through one side of the carburetor, but you cannot allow an air leak anywhere else—around a throttle shaft, for instance. Add to this the fact they are tough to clean and require trial-and-error adjustments. Restoring carburetors well is a little more involved than what it might seem at first glance.

These photographs outline work performed by two of the top carburetor shops in the John Deere Two-Cylinder world: Robert's Carburetor Repair and Burrey Carburetor Service. Both are reputable, do thorough, excellent work, and are very involved with the John Deere tractor collecting and restoration pastime. In all of the photographs you will note how meticulous these shops

are, paying careful attention to every detail. The results you see, unless otherwise mentioned, are not special one-off repairs. Every carb that passes through these shops receives this kind of care, and sets the standard for carburetor restoration; this is the standard you should set for your own work. Both shops stock parts, diagrams, videos, and other resources to help with your project. Their contact information also can be found in the appendices.

Tips & Tricks

• When restoring a carburetor, keep in mind that passageways must be crystal clean, jets should be like new, and float-level settings are the most critical areas. One common source of trouble is modern cleaning solution: The newer, water-based cleaners have enough surface tension to stay in and clog passageways if a drop is left behind. Be sure to use compressed air to blow out all passageways before assembly.

RESTORING A CARBURETOR

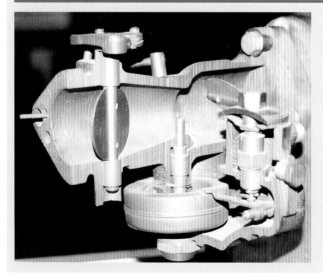

Visitors to Robert's Carburetor Repair will find this cut-away carburetor on the front counter. At the center right of the photograph you can see the vertical chamber into which the fuel enters the carburetor. The fuel fills this chamber, then falls into the bowl through the top of the brass fitting, above the strainer. This strains the gas on its way down into the bowl where the ring float (at lower center) turns on and off the flow of gas based on fuel level in the bowl. The air rushing into the carburetor is compressed through the narrowed passage (seen in the middle of the photograph), which in turn creates a low-pressure zone that draws fuel up through the main nozzle, shown here rising vertically through the float. This fuel is mixed with the air and the mixture is drawn into the engine. While this is a simplified description of how a carburetor works, it's not overly simplified. A well-tuned carburetor has only a few attributes: It keeps just the right amount of fuel in the bowl, has open and smooth passages for the flow of fuel, is adjusted correctly for the tractor it is installed on, and doesn't leak fuel. I'll detail a carburetor to help you understand how to properly adjust your carburetor.

Here are a few examples of unusual carburetors. At top left is an early brass carburetor from a Model G. The one above is quite rare, and is a full brass carburetor from a Waterloo Boy. To the left is a carburetor from the diesel pony starter engine. When restoring your diesel tractors, don't forget to restore these carburetors.

Here are two manifold-warming valves with only one difference between them: The first one works and the second one is stuck beyond repair. Unless you love challenges that waste hours of your time, loosening stuck valves is definitely not worth the time; replacement valves are available.

RESTORING A CARBURETOR (CONTINUED)

To remove your carburetor, remove the bolts that mount it to the manifold. Trying to take off the air cleaner tube and hose first is the hard way to remove the carburetor. You only have to remove the hose clamp and work the hose off the air-cleaner outlet. The second picture shows the entire assembly removed and resting on the tractor's frame.

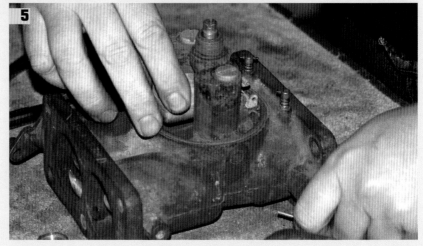

Next, disassemble the carburetor by removing the bowl (3). Doug Burrey of Burrey Carburetor Repair removes the pin the float pivots on (4). Then he removes the float.

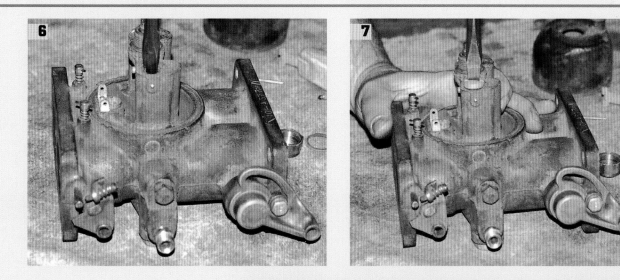

Remove all the plugs and the jet from the main nozzle area of the carburetor. Doug Burrey starts with the main nozzle area of the carburetor. These three photographs (6-9) show the plugs and jets you need to find and remove.

This plug needs to come out to expose passages that require cleaning.

Remove the throttle plates by removing the two screws that hold each plate to the throttle shaft.

Engine Systems Restoration and Testing

With the plates off, the shaft can be pulled out.

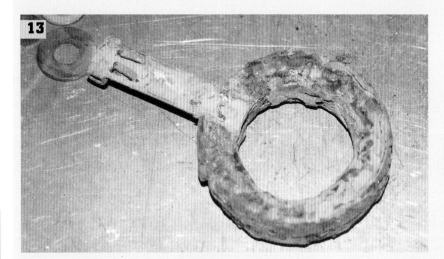

This sequence of photographs shows you some of the problems you may encounter when you disassemble your carburetor. If your float looks like this, you'll need to get a new one. Most floats are not in this bad of shape, and unless your float has a hole in it or is damaged, you can reuse it. To check for a hole, shake it and listen for fuel inside. If can't hear fuel, then submerge it as deep under water as possible and look for air bubbles coming out of the float. If it passes these tests, you can reuse it.

I don't even know what happened to this one, but I couldn't believe what kind of crud and nastiness had worked its way into this bowl when I first saw it. Rust also has run rampant.

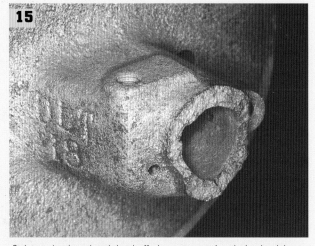

Carburetor bowl nut threads break off when water gets into the bowl and then freezes. This one is broken above the threads and requires a machine shop repair.

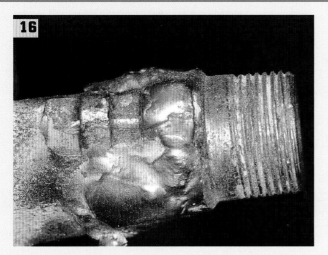

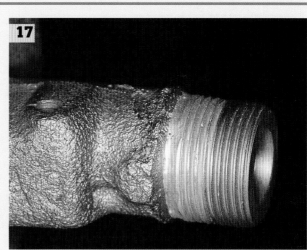

Here is a thread that has been broken and repaired. The roughness of the repair and the close proximity of important jets and passages would cause me to have this unit repaired properly.

Here is a broken bowl-nut thread that has been properly repaired. The brazing is tight and minimal, the threads have been cut cleanly and no passages have been compromised. Robert's Carburetor Repair repaired this thread.

After removing all of the plugs, jets and parts from the carburetor, give it a good washing in a parts washer.

Next, using a bead media, blast the carburetor body clean. Do NOT perform this step if you are not committed to thoroughly cleaning each passageway. Media will be left behind in these passages after this step, which isn't a problem if you drill each passageway to remove all accumulated crud and media particles.

RESTORING A CARBURETOR (CONTINUED)

After blasting, the carburetor body should look this clean.

The manifold mating surface of carburetors will warp over time. This carburetor body is being milled to return the mating surface to true.

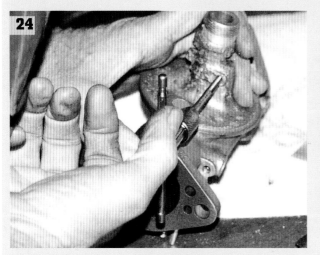

These four photographs show the various passageways that should be reamed or drilled. Care must be taken to be sure the drill or ream is oriented properly, and that you don't drill a blind passageway too far.

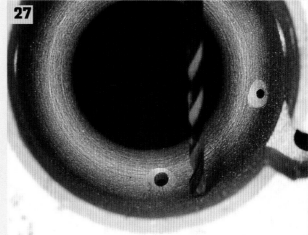

Throttle-shaft bushings should be replaced; here, Doug Burrey drives in a new one.

After the bushing is installed, you will need to ream it to size.

Most John Deere carburetors were painted, save the early brass-throat carburetors, and even then, the bowls were painted. A quick shot of paint is all that is needed to finish the carburetor; there is no need for primers or other coatings.

Shown is an assortment of N.O.S. and reproduction throttle shaft arms and whole throttle shafts. These are sold through Burrey Carburetor, along with the varnish-coated cork floats [4-42], that are required on early carburetors if your restoration is painfully accurate.

RESTORING A CARBURETOR (CONTINUED)

Assembly of your carburetor means putting together a collection of replacement parts, and parts that you removed from your carburetor and cleaned for reuse. Don't forget the water manifold if your tractor has one (the large brass piece, middle-right).

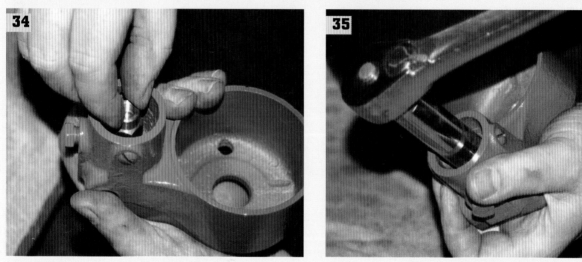

Start the assembly process by installing the bowl. First, install the float needle seat; tighten it down well (35), then put a new strainer on the fuel inlet chamber cap (36) and install the cap (37).

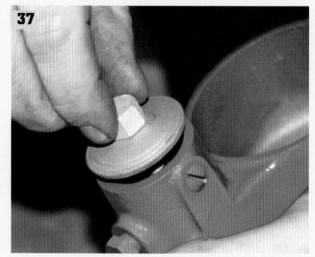

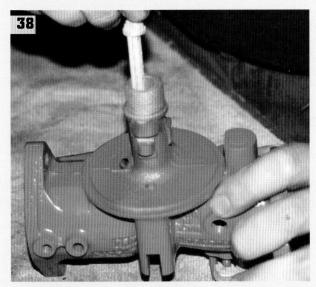

Next, install the main nozzle—there is a gasket that should first be placed in the nozzle passage.

Installing the throttle-shaft dust seal is easiest if you install it on the shaft instead of in front of the bushing in the throttle shaft bore. Next, slide in the shaft (40), and work the seal into place (41).

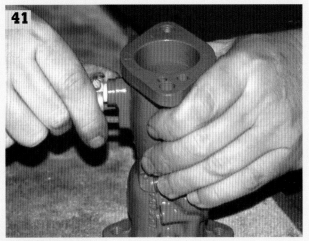

Attach the throttle-shaft plate with new screws. The throttle shaft should now turn easily and freely without binding.

RESTORING A CARBURETOR (CONTINUED)

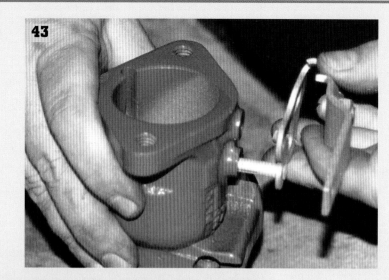

The choke shaft is installed almost the same way as the throttle shaft.

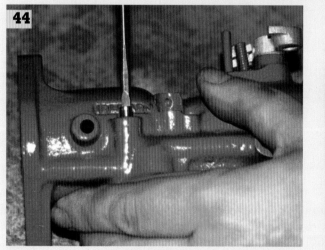

The remainder of the assembly involves installing the last of the jets and plugs, the mixture and idle speed adjusting screws (45), and attaching the bowl to the carburetor.

After assembly, you need to adjust, set up, and test your carburetor. First, mount the carburetor on the tractor. Replace the bowl drain with a small nozzle, attach a clear plastic line to the nozzle, and route the tube upwards. Attach the fuel line to the carburetor, and open the fuel flow. Watch the level of the fuel in the tube. The fuel should remain below the top of the bowl at a distance that matches your carburetor's float level specification; your manual should have this specification. You can check this specification with a ruler as you are assembling the carburetor, but the method shown is the most accurate.

MODIFIED CARBURETORS

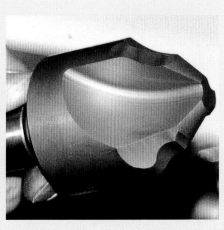

Getting more performance out of your John Deere is the goal of many people, especially folks who will use their tractors competitively in tractor pulls or plowing matches. The most widely used modified carburetor is one from Robert's Carburetor Repair. Initially, Robert's set out to address this need by testing various modifications to fuel and airflow rates. Their new modified carburetors, when compared to stock carburetors, increase airflow and, consequently, fuel flow into the engine. An engine with these modified carburetors just simply "breathes" better. Creating these specifications took some research, and trial and error. First, volumetric and other airflow data were collected from stock carburetors and various initial designs using the device pictured at top left, which measures airflow and vacuum. After creating a set of specifications that created a significant increase in horsepower, tooling, such as the profile cutter (above), had to be created to faithfully reproduce the design. To actually create a carburetor, Robert chucks the carburetor into a latheand machines the throat. The profile cutter and additional machining creates a throat profile to Robert's new, high-performance specifications (below).

(continued on page 80)

MODIFIED CARBURETORS (CONTINUED)

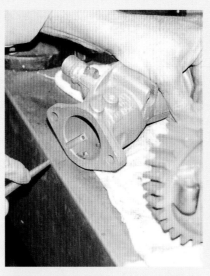

The differences between a stock and a modified carburetor can be seen in the photograph directly above. After additional machine work, the freshly milled and cut surfaces are dressed with a file, if needed (top, center), and the carburetor is fully rebuilt. The carburetor is mounted on a test tractor next (top, right) The test tractor is attached to a dynamometer that measures how much extra power each modified carburetor is putting out. After engine warm up and carburetor adjustment, the dynamometer is spun up (right), and the testing is started.

DIESEL FUEL INJECTION

This photograph shows the diesel-fuel injection body for a Model R. This is the housing that holds the entire system and bolts it up to the tractor. These diesel fuel injection rebuild photographs are not provided to encourage you to rebuild these yourself, rather, to give you a little background information and familiarity with these systems. Unless you have specific training in this area and the proper equipment, diesel fuel system restoration should always be farmed out to professionals. In these photographs Central Fuel Injection (found in the appendices) technicians step us through the process.

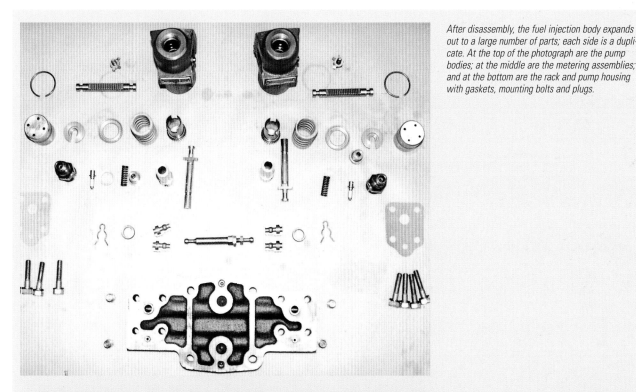

After disassembly, the fuel injection body expands out to a large number of parts; each side is a duplicate. At the top of the photograph are the pump bodies; at the middle are the metering assemblies; and at the bottom are the rack and pump housing with gaskets, mounting bolts and plugs.

Shown is a packing ring that is inside the diesel fuel-pump body. Originally, these rings were copper. Since they were housed in a pump body made of steel, electrolytic corrosion caused erosion of these rings. Over time, the erosion was significant enough to leave the tractor disabled. Steel rings were introduced as a fix, but not until a large number of tractors had problems. For accuracy, copper is being used again in this restoration. Because the tractor will not see heavy work again, the return to copper is acceptable.

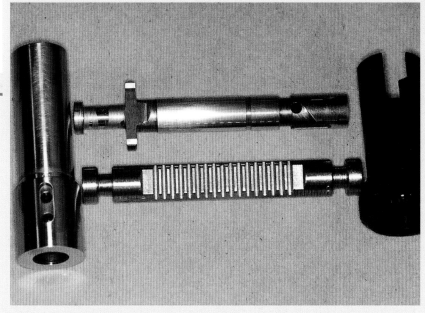

These parts from the diesel fuel-injection system are responsible for determining the flow of fuel to the engine. On the bottom rod, called a rack, you can see the graduations used to adjust fuel flow rate.

DIESEL FUEL INJECTION (CONTINUED)

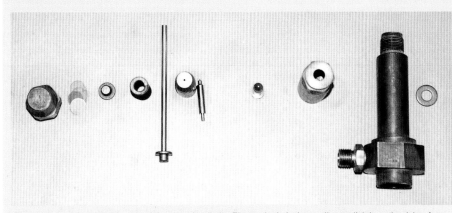

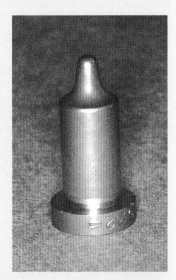

Shown are the injector-nozzle assemblies at each cylinder. The nozzle tip is the small part slightly to the right of center and is also shown close-up in the next photograph. The picture to the right shows a close-up of the tip. These nozzle tips are incredibly delicate. In many models of Deere diesels, the injector tip extends below the bottom plane of the cylinder head; and is easy to damage if you don't remove the nozzles from the cylinder heads before removing the head. This is one of the most common causes of injector tip damage.

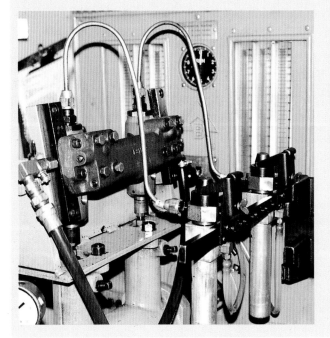

Mounted to a test stand is the diesel fuel injection system of a John Deere R; pump pressure, injector tip spray pattern and flow rate are tested. The picture above is a photograph of the back of the diesel fuel injection system. You can see the end of one of the racks, and an adjusting nut. Flow rate can be adjusted, but pressure is indicative of the health of the pump; poor spray patterns require a new injector nozzle tip.

Restoring magnetos requires a fundamental understanding of how they work. The John Deere manual, *Tractors and Engines (General)*, covers the fundamentals, but I'll explain a few of the nitty-gritty details.

Let's start with two premises scientists discovered more than a hundred years ago, which that industry has been taking advantage of since: A magnetic field that crosses a wire creates an electrical current. The amount of current produced in the wire by a magnetic field depends on the number of times the magnetic field intersects a single continuous wire. Conversely, when an electrical current is produced, the current creates a magnetic field. The magneto is simply a device that harnesses these two theories.

A magneto spins a magnet in the presence of a conductor (wire). This conductor may actually take on the form of a metal bar or something similar instead of wire, but the idea is identical. The wire or conductor, called the primary winding, creates a magnetic field. When the current in the primary winding is turned "off," the magnetic field it has created collapses and crosses through a group of fine, tightly wound wires called the secondary wiring. This secondary wiring is usually packaged in a weatherproof coating, called a coil. The wire in the coil is wrapped thousands of times resulting in something that looks like a small, tall, doughnut. Every wrap increases the number of times the magnetic field crosses it, thereby increasing the voltage.

When the magnetic field crosses the coil during its collapse, a high-voltage current is created in the coil. This current is discharged through the rotor cap, spark plug wire, and then ultimately through the spark plug where a spark is created in the cylinder. Everything else in the magneto synchronizes the spark to the engine: The breaker points turn the current in the primary winding on and off to create the collapse of the magnetic field around the primary winding at just the right time. The impulse coupling delays the spark for slow engine speeds, such as at startup. Some magnetos spin the primary wiring, and the magnets are stationary. Even though every magneto is a little different, in the end, they all operate by these two premises.

Knowing and understanding how magnetos work helps in their restoration. You should realize that the coil is responsible for delivering a hot spark to the engine. A bad coil will often fail to create a spark, or occasionally fail to create a spark after it warms up from the constant discharging of high-voltage current. Cracks and deterioration in the coating mean moisture from the air may ground all or part of the coil against itself, rendering it inoperable until it dries. Unless it appears that the coil has been replaced in the recent past, a new coil is a must for every magneto restoration.

Other areas that need attention are the magnets, mechanical assembly, and impulse coupling and breaker-point assembly. The mechanical assembly—the magneto shaft and armature—should get new bearings and seals. The impulse coupling will likely need cleaning, light oiling, and a possible repair or two, and the magnets should be recharged to ensure a strong current through the primary winding. After cleaning the rest of the unit and replacing the breaker points, rotor cap, and spark plug wire, you should set the breaker point gap. After this is done, you are ready to test.

To test, mount the magneto in a vise; be sure wood or some other insulator keeps the base of the magneto from touching the metal of the vise. Then insert a spark plug wire in a plug terminal on the cap and carefully hold the wire close to the base of the magneto, without touching it. Spin up the magneto with a variable-speed drill. It might require a bit of ingenuity to rig this up. I use a spare magneto coupling disc with a rod attached that I can chuck into the drill. When the magneto is turning, look for a good clean spark jumping from the spark plug wire to the base of the magneto. The spark should be reasonably bright, blue, and able to jump a gap that is about .040-.060 inch. To finish, leave the unit unpainted for the time being, and mount it to the tractor following service manual recommendations.

Although not the easiest part of the restoration, a magneto rebuild will certainly enhance the running characteristics of your tractor, even if the magneto was acceptable beforehand. A strong, well-controlled spark is critical to power delivery.

Tips & Tricks

• There are three keys to magneto restoration: recharging the magnets, installing a new coil, and making sure that both the low-voltage side (primary windings) and the high-voltage side (the coil) and their associated leads are well insulted from the magneto base. Although other areas like points, adjustment, cleaning, bearings, and seals are important, these areas are the most critical to restoring a magneto to top performance.

This is what a magneto looks like after disassembling and cleaning. Notice that all parts are extremely clean, without any remaining rust or corrosion. This is important if you want your magneto restoration to last a long time.

After cleaning, virtually all metal parts in the magneto should receive a light coating of silicone spray. This will help keep them from developing corrosion or rust after the restoration.

Any bushings inside the stator shaft should be replaced unless you are sure the current bushings are in excellent shape.

All gaskets and seals should be replaced during a restoration; here are a few gaskets to be used in restoration.

Old seals are often a different size than modern seals, creating a dilemma: How do you find a replacement? Here, Robert's Carburetor Repair solves the problem by trimming down a modern seal on a lathe so it fits.

Small touches make the restoration authentic. Here knobs used to attach a grounding kill wire are replaced with original knobs.

The heart of every magneto repair is the recharging of the magnets. A magnet's ability to create a magnetic field diminishes over time, especially if there has been a long period of disuse. A magneto charger isn't something you'll likely have sitting around, but an electrical motor repair shop in your town might have one. Plans for building one are available at dozens of places on the Internet, too.

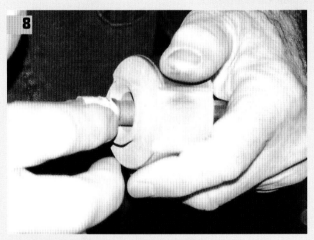

The stator shaft should be lightly coated with assembly grease before placing it into the body of the magneto.

In addition to the assembly grease, place a small drop of oil anywhere the stator rubs, such as on a thrust washer or a bushing shoulder.

The stator slides into the body of the magneto; check for fit between the stator shaft and the new bushing.

The oil felt, which is replaced during a magneto refurbishment, is saturated with a moderate amount of oil. The felt shouldn't be sloppy wet, but there should be enough oil to evenly saturate the felt. The amount seen here is just about right.

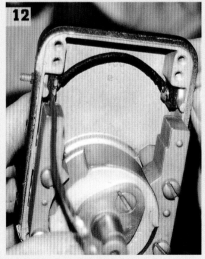

The kill wire terminals have been reinsulated, and new wiring is installed between them. If your magneto has a ground kill terminal, don't forget to attach the lead from the points to the terminal.

RESTORING A MAGNETO (CONTINUED)

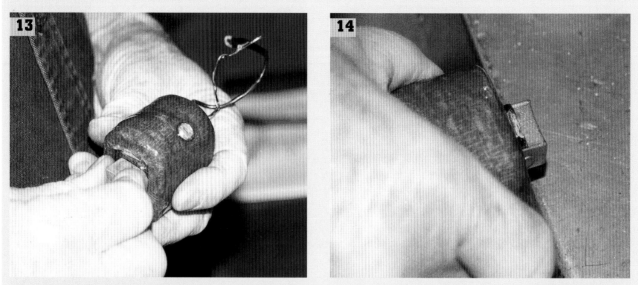

A new coil should always be installed during any magneto refurbishment. In the first photograph, the iron core for the coil is fitted in place. In the second, small wedges are driven in to hold the bar in place.

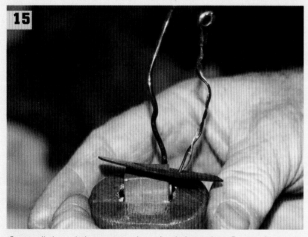

Some coils have their own protective or insulating gaskets. Be sure they are installed.

The iron bar is placed on the field magnets (16), and clips are installed (17) to hold it in place.

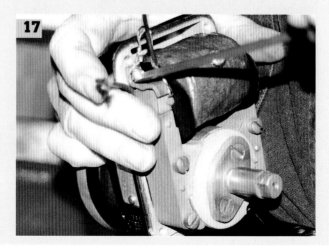

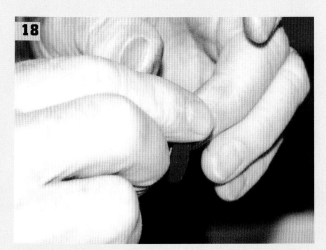

Before driving in any seal, including magneto seals, coat the outside edge with oil. This seal was meant to keep things *out* of the magneto. The seal is installed so the spring side of the seal faces the tractor, not the rest of the magneto.

The plate and seal is installed in the magneto. Again, notice the orientation. This orientation keeps debris, such as excessive oil from the drive coupling of the governor, out of the magneto. It is *not* oriented to keep things in the magneto.

Mount the plate to the magneto body. Any time bolts are installed, it makes sense to first clean out the bolt holes with a tap, as seen here, before installing the bolt.

Tighten down the bolts, remembering that magneto bodies are usually pot metal and therefore soft; high-torque values do not belong here.

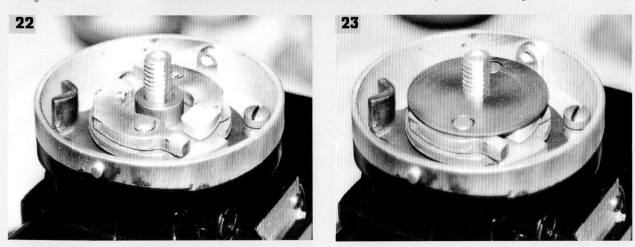

Finish assembling the impulse assembly, making sure each item has been covered with the silicone spray.

RESTORING A MAGNETO (CONTINUED)

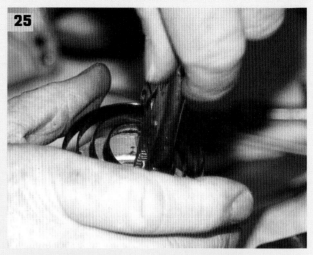

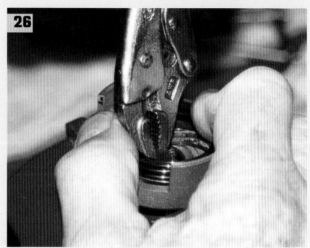

This group of shots shows the installation of the impulse coupling spring and drive coupling. Anyone who has installed the spring in pull-start lawnmowers knows how this works. Start by mounting the drive coupling in a suitable vice and mount the outside end of the spring in the drive coupling (24) Then wind the spring by hand; needle-nose vice grips are handy for this step (25 & 26). Oil the spring (27), then install the spring boss into the drive coupling and seat the other end of the spring in its anchor (28). This magneto uses a slot, but it might be a pin on the impulse assembly depending on the make and model of magneto. If needed, make sure the spring is wound a few turns and install the drive coupling on the shaft (29) Secure with a fastener (30). You are done with the drive part of the magneto. Next, we'll turn our attention to the high-tension side.

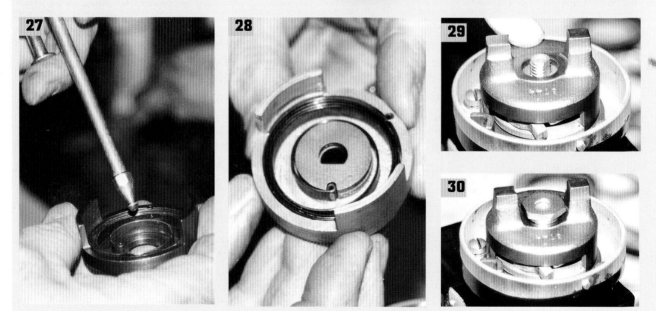

The remainder of the restoration involves installing the front end of the magneto, such as the points. Obviously, all-new components should be used, including plug wires and rotor tower. Here, the points and condenser are being installed.

Make sure the kill wire, condenser wire and coil wire are installed together and secured tightly.

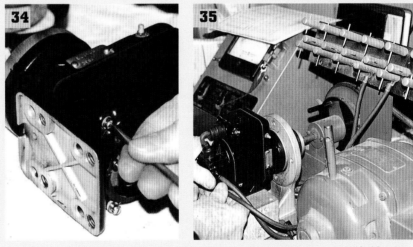

Adjust the point gap and take the time to be accurate and careful. Add just a dab of point lube at the trailing edge of the point's cam follower.

Fit the cover to the magneto and test the magneto. Here is a professional magneto test stand [35] But, an extra set of hands, a variable speed drill, a homemade drive coupling, an ungrounded vice to hold the magneto, and a little ingenuity and creativity will test the magneto just fine. Remember, these things bite. Be sure you are not the ground path for a magneto if you hate unpleasant shocks!

The finished product. Restoring magnetos is a bit involved and time-consuming and nearly impossible for the novice to do correctly without a little help from a professional or friend. But, it is not rocket science, and can be done by a weekend mechanic who has a solid dose of aptitude, persistence, and a little help. John Deere's book on engine systems, SM-200, has a great section on magnetos and is a must-read before starting.

You can restore a distributor yourself; these systems are simple and are no more difficult than anything else you've tackled thus far. There are three areas of a distributor that need attention during a restoration. They are the drive shaft bushing, the centrifugal-advance mechanism, and the integrity of the high-voltage delivery components. To begin disassembly, start by removing the distributor cap, the rotor tower (the plastic piece that distributes the spark to the spark plug cables), and the dust cap that covers the points and the condenser. Remove the points and condenser and then the mounting plate of the points and condenser. Remove all terminals and insulators from the body of the distributor. Check the condition of the insulators and replace any that look even a little bit worn or damaged. Removing the points mounting plate exposes the centrifugal-advance mechanism. The springs should be removed first and set aside, then the weights and centrifugal-advance shaft will lift off the drive shaft and out of the distributor body after loosening a couple of keeper nuts.

Next, turn your attention to the drive shaft. Spin the shaft by hand, trying to feel for any looseness, bind, abnormal noises, or rubbing sensations. If the shaft spins freely but not loosely, and without any sensation of grinding or rubbing, you can then thoroughly clean all of the components and reassemble. If there is considerable looseness in the drive shaft or any sound or sensation that concerns you, follow a few more steps and remove the drive shaft from the distributor and replace the bushing(s) found in the body of the distributor that the shaft rides in.

To remove the shaft, turn the distributor on its side and drive out the pin that holds the drive coupling to the shaft. The drive shaft can then be gently driven out of the gear from the top of the distributor. To renew the bushing, first press out the old bushing of the distributor body from the bottom (distributor body upside down) using a shop press and an arbor that is suitably sized to prevent damage to the distributor body. A new bushing is available from some NOS parts dealers, found in the appendices. Press in the new bushing. A well-stocked local machine shop can make a custom bushing for you and handle the pressing work, too. Reassembly of the distributor is the opposite of the disassembly; keep in mind the following important information.

The drive coupling's flange (the ridge along the bottom of the coupling) is slightly offset. When installing the coupling to the shaft, be sure the coupling is indexed correctly to the shaft. To do this, hold the distributor upright, with the shaft in the body, the centrifugal-advance mechanism on the shaft and the rotor tower on the top, and turn the shaft so the tower tip points toward you. Then place the coupling in the shaft and rotate the coupling so the pinhole in the shaft and the coupling line up and the flange is offset to the left. When installing the pin, be sure to peen over the top of the pin to create a rivet head on both sides of the pin. This is important in preventing the pin from falling out during operation.

The points, condenser, distributor rotor tip, and distributor cap should all be replaced during reassembly. Any terminal that looks less than perfect should be replaced and all insulators should be replaced. Some insulators have a special shape and will have to be purchased from a parts source. The wafer- and washer-shaped insulators can be made from insulting material found at electronic stores. Be sure to oil the distributor with 30-weight oil; be very careful not to overoil. The service manual for your tractor will show you where the oil hole for your particular model is, but most have a small screw-in plug in which you place oil.

Distributor restoration starts with the removal of the unit from your tractor.

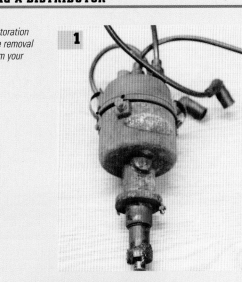

Removal of the distributor cap, dust seal and rotor tower, shown off of the distributor, begins the disassembly.

This is the inertial advance mechanism, disassembled.

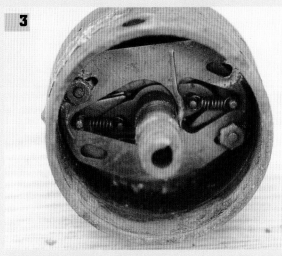

Next comes the removal of the inertial advance mechanism. I like to take it off at this point by removing the two springs, then the two nuts, and then the locking collars of the nuts. Be sure to first bend their tags out of the way.

To remove the rotor shaft from the distributor housing, you must first remove the drive pin. To remove the drive pin, grind off both peened ends. Care should be taken to minimize damage to the drive coupling, though some grinding marks and scratches are to be expected.

To remove the drive pin, remove the heads from the pin on both sides. A small grinder and careful grinding will remove the heads without damaging the body or the drive coupling.

The drive pin removal continues by drilling the pin out. In this picture, I've already drilled the pin and pressed the shaft in a small arbor press to shear what is left of the pin. To prevent damaging the shaft, drill out only that part of the pin that resides in the drive coupling. Stop as soon as the drill bit has gone far enough to be passing into the shaft. Chuck the distributor housing into a press and begin pressing the rotor shaft out of the coupling. If you have drilled just far enough, what little bit of the pin is left at the coupling/shaft junction will shear easily and the shaft will come down through the coupling.

Removing the rest of the pin requires a small punch; at this point it should come right out.

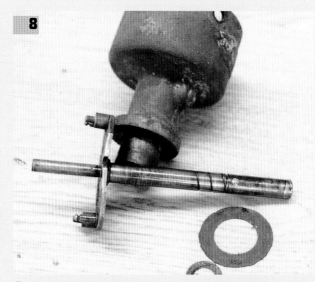

The rotor shaft is removed from the housing. You can see the remnant of the pin still in the shaft; I was careful to retrieve the thrust washer from inside the body of the distributor. The larger washer is actually a gasket I missed when I removed the distributor from the tractor; it was stuck on the bottom at the base.

Inside the distributor body, you can see the thrust washer, and you get a good view of the top edge of the bushing that the rotor shaft rides in. This bushing almost always needs to be replaced. Now is the time to remove the screw on the side of the distributor that is used to oil the bushing.

A lot simpler than a magneto, and devoid of any insurmountable challenges, the distributor is something you can, and should, restore yourself. A little bit of common sense and help from a machine shop to create and/or press a bushing and peen over a drive pin, will get you through the process. After parts replacement, assembly is exactly in reverse of assembly with one exception: You might find it easier to install the inertial advance mechanism onto the drive shaft before you insert the drive shaft into the distributor body.

After the engine is assembled, test it before doing any painting or further assembly of the tractor. To test, verify that the carburetor or diesel pump and injection systems, cooling, and spark delivery systems are present, restored, and installed. Equally important is the ability to shut off the engine. Make sure you have a temporary kill switch installed if the normal kill switch is not yet installed (a ground tab on the magneto or distributor, or a lanyard attached to the fuel cutoff on the diesel systems). Using this book and your service manual, verify all connections and mentally double- and triple-check everything. Before starting the engine, prime the oil-pressure system by turning over the engine with the fuel and ignition switched off. Continue doing this until oil pressure rises. Once it rises, turn on the fuel and ignition and try to start the tractor. If your tractor is a diesel, be sure the diesel fuel-injection system is primed, the filters are new, and the water traps are clean.

If your tractor doesn't start, work your way through the engine using standard diagnostic tools and procedures. Two of the most likely culprits are fuel and ignition delivery failures. (Newly rebuilt engines typically generate the needed compression, the third condition needed for quick starting.) Verify that the engine timing is not off (magneto or distributor installed 180 degrees off is common) and that fuel is flowing to the carburetor bowl by opening the bowl drain. Continued starting problems shouldn't dissuade you from concentrating on fuel and ignition. Although it is possible the new engine may be at fault (failure to install cam followers/tappets is a mistake I have seen a time or two), new-engine starting problems are almost always traced to fuel and ignition. Check and double-check every part and component, if needed. I feel confident your problem can be found in these two areas.

Once you get it started, keep a close eye on oil pressure for a few minutes. While doing this, keep your ears tuned for abnormal sounds. If nothing is amiss, take the time to make the most of your rough adjustments to the carburetor and governor linkage. If all is well, keep the engine running for about 15 minutes. Vary the throttle setting occasionally, staying away from maximum throttle setting for now. After 15 minutes, shut down the engine and let it cool. Retorque the head bolts and install the valve cover with fresh sealant.

Congratulations, you've restored a John Deere engine! This is the point that probably excites me the most during a restoration. A brand-new, purring engine means the restoration is well on its way. No matter what happens or doesn't happen from here on out, finishing this step means you've accomplished something; you've saved another tractor. It means that an important piece of our agri-industrial heritage is now in better condition than it was before. These are not small accomplishments and a little pride and self-satisfaction is deserved. Savor this moment, because you still have a lot work to do on the cosmetic restoration. Before moving forward, clean any gasket sealant, grease, or oil from the outside surfaces of the engine.

After assembling the engine you should test it before any more cosmetic work is done. Here, a small gas tank supplies the gas needed for a test run of the engine. You won't need to install the hood and/or tank just to test the engine, because it will have to be removed again for restoration or last minute changes and fixes to the engine.

5

Transmission and Drivetrain Restoration

"(God) lives as comfortably in … the gears of a transmission as he does at the top of a mountain or in the petals of a flower."
—Robert M. Pirsig

Restoring the transmission and drivetrain of your John Deere tractor is probably the most expensive part of the restoration. Because of the precision and close tolerances of these parts and systems, in addition to the force required to disassemble some of them, it can be the most exasperating, and also time consuming. Typically, I can restore two engines in the time it takes to perform one transmission and drivetrain restoration. However, nothing makes a larger difference to a tractor's overall drivability, creates such a sense of "newness," and more authoritatively ends any argument questioning whether your restoration was "complete." If powertrain restoration is something your tractor needs, then let's jump right in.

REMOVING THE WHEELS

REAR WHEELS

Removal of all types of rear wheels starts with the draining of liquid ballast, and the removal of any weights. Because rear tractor wheels can be heavy even after the draining of all ballast, be sure to have someone help you with removal. Bolt-on wheels are not difficult to remove; these types of wheels will come off the axle flange with only moderate levels of persuasion, even in the worst cases, after unbolting them. Sliding the wheels off adjustable axles (long, rod-type axles) can be tough, and tremendous force and patience are required. If you have a tractor with adjustable wheels, remove any paint, grease, or dirt from that part of the axle outside of the wheels; then apply grease to the axle. For safety reasons, the tractor's entire rear end should be supported during this operation rather than supporting only the end you are working on. Loosen the wheel hubs that clamp the wheel onto the axle and apply penetrating oil to the area where the wheel hub and axle meet. Next, apply copious amounts of heat using a gas-welding outfit that has a heating tip installed. The heat will help loosen the hub from the axle.

Begin moving the wheels outward with whatever means you have at your disposal. I use a homemade contraption that will usually get the wheel moving without damaging it. The pictures show this better than I can explain. The puller in the photographs was made, and is being demonstrated by Herb Nielsen of Nielsen Spoke Wheel Repair (see the appendices). Something similar can be shop-made by you, or by a fabrication shop. This type of press is designed to get the wheel moving, which is the toughest part. Once moving, a variety of standard pullers, winches, and elbow grease can usually get the wheel and hub off the remainder of the axle. If worse comes to worst, the wheel press pictured will work the wheel all the way off, though it is tedious and time consuming. Be sure you have the tractor well supported during the entire operation.

With the tires dismounted, the rear wheels can be assessed for restoration possibilities. Local metal fabrication and repair shops can easily repair simple, small problems such as rust-out at the valve stem hole. Most damage or heavy rust on rear wheels is tough to safely repair. In addition, some of the pressed or stamped rear wheels are less expensive to replace with good used wheels, even if they can be repaired. If your tractor has collectible, expensive spoke wheels, then you may find that repairs, even if they are expensive, are cheaper than replacement (if replacements are available at all). Only by shopping for replacements, or by sending pictures of the wheels to the various shops listed in the appendices, can you find out if your rear wheels should be salvaged or repaired.

Tips & Tricks

• When pulling off rear wheels, always fasten the puller to the hub of the wheel. Never pull on the spokes or disc of the rear wheel; you *will* damage the wheel.

REMOVING THE WHEELS

Removing rear wheels from these old tractors can be tough. Here, a homemade puller is mounted to help with the process. The steel plate is centered on the end of the axle, then bolts are threaded in the hub of the wheel. Heat and penetrating oil applied to the hub and slight turns of each bolt will ultimately free the wheel from the axle. There are a couple of interesting things to note: Notice the bolt orientation triangles. Each of the common wheel-hub bolt-hole patterns is drilled into the plate and a triangle is scribed between the bolt holes that belong to the same pattern. Notice, too, that hardened bolts are used for this task—five marks on the head of a bolt signify a grade 8 hardened bolt.

Repairing wheels that are difficult or expensive to replace requires the help of a machine shop. This round, rear spoke wheel has been milled in anticipation of being fitted with a custom-made hub. While expensive, it is cheaper than replacing the wheel.

Cracked hubs can be repaired with plate rings. While not as pretty as a welded repair, this repair is much safer and longer lasting. This is because welded hub cracks will often form again as soon as the taper lock hub is drawn tight. The taper lock hub has a flange, and therefore, the extra thickness of the ring is not as noticeable after installation of the wheel as it would seem from this picture.

When you start the rear axle restoration, the seal area probably looks like this, or worse. Clean the area well and begin by removing the retainer that holds a felt seal in place. There is a spacer on the backside of the felt seal that should be removed, too.

After the retainer is removed, the seal comes out. Behind it is a second retainer and a bearing spacer. The outboard axle bearing is slightly visible behind it.

This photograph shows the outboard rear axle bearing and spacer. It is likely it will need to be replaced because of the bearing's exposure to dirt and dust, and the fact that it should have been greased (on some models) and often wasn't.

Tips & Tricks

• Hydraulic jacks placed against the axle or transmission housings make a poor press when used for rear-wheel removal. They do make an acceptable puller when placed on the end of an axle to pull chains fastened to the hubs on the wheels.

• The differential bull gears can be reversed on most models of John Deere tractors. Reversing them moves the wear on these gears from the forward motion direction to the reverse direction. This will quiet the tractor in the forward direction (of course, now reverse movement will be as noisy as forward was before).

To remove the rear axles, loosen both of the inner axle nuts, and drive a soft steel, long-taper wedge between the inner ends of the axles. One of the axles will start moving outwards and can be taken out. Take care when driving this wedge; the hammer needed to get one of the axles moving has to be big, and misplaced blows have broken more than one differential bull-gear tooth. After the first axle is removed, the second can be driven out with a long, steel driving rod.

When the axle is moving, pull it the rest of the way out so the steel rod isn't bound under the weight of the bull gear. The bull gear is heavy and edges of the gear teeth are sharp, so be careful when handling it. It is safe to let it drop to the bottom of the housing. Pull out the gear, being sure to catch the bearing behind it (right). This inboard axle bearing is usually well lubricated by transmission fluid. Highly worn inboard bearings are not as common as their outboard counterparts.

FRONT AXLE

The front wheels are removed after the front of the tractor is raised up off the ground and supported by jacks under the frame support at the front of the tractor. Remove the wheels by removing the nut at the end of the wheel spindles. Pull the wheels straight off, being sure to catch the outside front wheel bearing and associated parts that may fall out; the wheels will come right off.

Roll-O-Matic assemblies can then be removed if your tractor is so equipped. The Roll-O-Matic assembly is secured with bolts to the housing at the end of the pedestal. After these bolts are removed, pull the two spindle sectors at the same time, straight out from the housing.

If the wheels themselves are in need of restoration or repair, now is the time to send those out to a restoration shop. Herb Nielsen of Nielsen Spoke Wheel Repair can take care of your front spoke wheels; most local machine shops can handle cast wheels or simple small repairs. Like rear wheels, pressed steel wheels can usually be replaced less expensively than they can be repaired if the damage or rust is extensive.

Restoration of the front end starts with a thorough cleaning of all parts, paying special attention to the inside of the front wheel hubs; they have probably never been cleaned in their entire life. Next, clean and inspect the front wheel bearings. These bearings tend to last a good long while and often can be successfully reused. Like all bearings, they should be replaced if they show any sign of fatigue, corrosion, or excessive wear. Inspect the spindles for cracks or damage, especially around their base. On wide front axles, check the fit and movement of the spindles inside the spindle housing; excessive looseness is dangerous and can affect steering. If the spindles are loose, the bushing inside the spindle housing will have to be replaced. To replace the bushing, disconnect the steering components and press the spindle out of the housing. Remove the axle from the tractor, press out the old bushing, and then press in a new one. Shop-grade presses are usually not up to this task, so you'll probably need the services of a professional shop for this step.

The sector gear teeth of the Roll-O-Matic spindle sectors are usually heavily worn, and the stops that limit the up-and-down travel are usually broken or worn. This means the spindle-sector gear will have to be replaced or repaired. Likewise, the tapered splines of many of the wide front axles have been stripped or damaged over the years. Mike Williams, listed in the appendices, specializes in repairing and remaking some front-end components for John Deere tractors, and can offer assistance with

FRONT AXLE RESTORATION

John Deere wheel restoration is an important part of your restoration, especially if your tractor has any of the rare and unusual wheels that collectors covet. Often the rims of these wheels are in bad shape and the spokes are bent or broken and have been welded. Herb Nielsen of Nielsen's spoke wheel repair can restore and repair just about any front wheel. In this sequence of photos, we'll touch on the highlights of his work. He starts by drilling out the spokes of the rim. Then, using a new rim from one of his suppliers, he mounts up the old hub and spoke assembly (above left). Using a fixture he intends to patent, he centers the hub and the spokes to the rim, and then draws them up in the fixture until the whole wheel is concentric. This fixture will create the nipples, and then he will weld the spokes back to the rim at these new nipples. Note how little difference there is between an original wheel (above right), and one of his wheels (below left). Finishing out the wheel restoration means verifying that you have the correct hub. At lower right is an unusual John Deere B front wheel hub.

spindles and sector gears. Last but not least, thoroughly inspect the axle or pedestal for any sign of cracks, damage, or wear that needs attention before assembly can commence.

Reassembly is the reverse of disassembly, but pay special attention to proper grease-packing procedures when assembling the front wheels. The Roll-O-Matic front end has to be reassembled so that the two spindle-sector halves are in register. This is not difficult, but easy to miss during reassembly. Other points of care during reassembly are thrust bearings (make sure they are installed in the correct orientation), and all spindles and bushings (make sure they are thoroughly greased before reassembly).

Tips & Tricks

• To remove the axles of Waterloo tractors, loosen the fastening nut of one of the axles, and then slowly drive a soft wedge between the interior ends of the axles. The axle nut that was loosened will start to drift out. After removal of the first axle, the other axle can be removed by removing its fastening nut first. Then press it out with a long steel drift inserted in the empty axle housing of the first axle, and drive the second axle out with a sledgehammer.

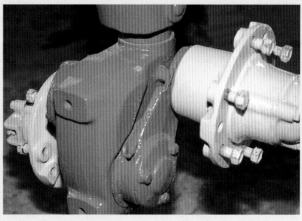

Restoration of the front end of a narrow-front John Deere begins with the removal of the front wheels. After adequately supporting the front end of the tractor, remove the wheel from the hub. Remove the hub by taking off the hubcap and the spindle nut that holds the hub on. The hub, bearing seals and dust shields will all come off. Tractors without Roll-O-Matic front ends now only need typical bearing replacement, cleaning and greasing to prepare for assembly, but those with Roll-O-Matic front ends have additional steps. The disassembly of the unit begins with removing the knuckle caps. At that point, remove the bolts through a lock plate and the thrust washers behind them. Each Roll-O-Matic knuckle can be pulled straight out. Restoration usually includes the replacement of the bushings in the knuckles, and machining to clean up the sector gear portion of the knuckle. The picture at top right illustrates the tremendous wear these gears often exhibit. Machine shops in your area, or Mike Williams, can build the gear face back up and cut it back to like-new dimensions.

BRAKES

The brakes of most John Deere tractors are very similar in construction, and the following general procedures can see you through the task. Removal of the entire braking unit on each side is straightforward and simple on most tractors. Fully and completely disassemble and clean each braking unit. Unless the brake pads are in exceptional shape, they should be replaced. The pads and shoes can also be replaced in their entirety with ready-made units, or you can remove the pads yourself and install new ones; the photographs in this chapter show you how. After cleaning, all fulcrum and contact points of the parts and assemblies should be coated with a compound designed to prevent the seizing of parts (Never-Seize is one compound that is available). Any rollers found in your brake system should be freed up. Lightly oil their rotation points and coat their circumference with an antiseizing compound. Be sure to coat all adjusting pins and bolts with an anti-seizing compound,

REPLACING BRAKE PADS

Replacing brake pads requires three simple tools: a rivet punch, a small hammer and a rivet anvil. Start by removing the brake pads and putting them in a well-ventilated spot (old pads probably have asbestos in them). The old pads have to come off first (2). Drilling out the rivets to remove the pads is possible if you trust your ability to drill dead-center. New rivets won't hold if the holes are widened through errant drilling. After the pads are removed, use a cold chisel to remove the heads of the rivets (3). With the rivets off, you can then clean, sandblast and spray a protective coating on the shoe.

making sure not to get this compound on the brake pads. If your brake unit has an oil seal, that should be replaced now.

At this point the brakes are ready to install on the tractor. After installation, replace or repair any brake linkage, pedal, or pedal bushing that shows wear. Some brake parts, such as the brake pedal locks, are often missing. Be sure to check your tractor's parts diagram for parts that are missing and replace them.

Tips & Tricks

• Have brake drums "turned" (the process of removing all blemishes from the braking surface) by a brake shop when restoring your brakes.

Once cleaned, install the pads by lining up the shoe and pad and placing a rivet through them (4). Back the rivet with the anvil, and using the rivet punch, draw the rivet tight against the pad. Turn over your work to verify that the rivet punch is solid and well centered (5). After installing the pad, oil the rollers and cover the operating surfaces with an anti-seize product. Install the springs (6). It is recommended that new springs be used at every pad replacement. All that is left to do now is to install them on the tractor.

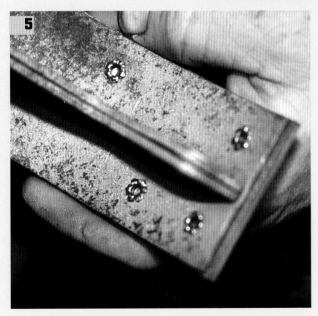

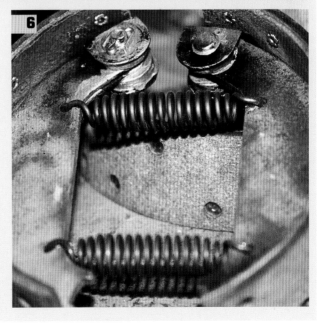

Brake system rebuilding begins by removing the brake drum. Remove the nut that holds the drum to the brake shaft, then take off the drum. This shows the right brake of a Model 60 after the drum has been removed.

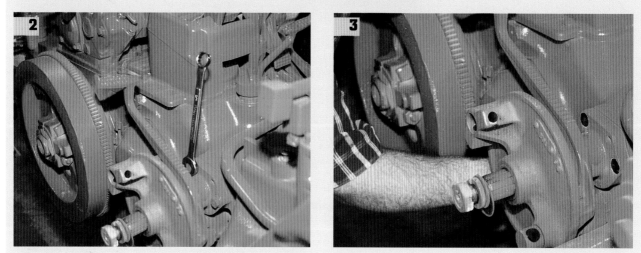

Next, remove the entire brake unit from the tractor. After removing a couple of mounting bolts, just pulling the unit will remove it from the tractor, but just as often, a little persuasion is necessary. Using a piece of wood to protect the brake housing (4), light taps with a mallet should get the unit moving out of the tractor. Lift the brake housing off the shaft (6). Again, a little tapping with a mallet on the outside end of the shaft may be necessary to get things moving.

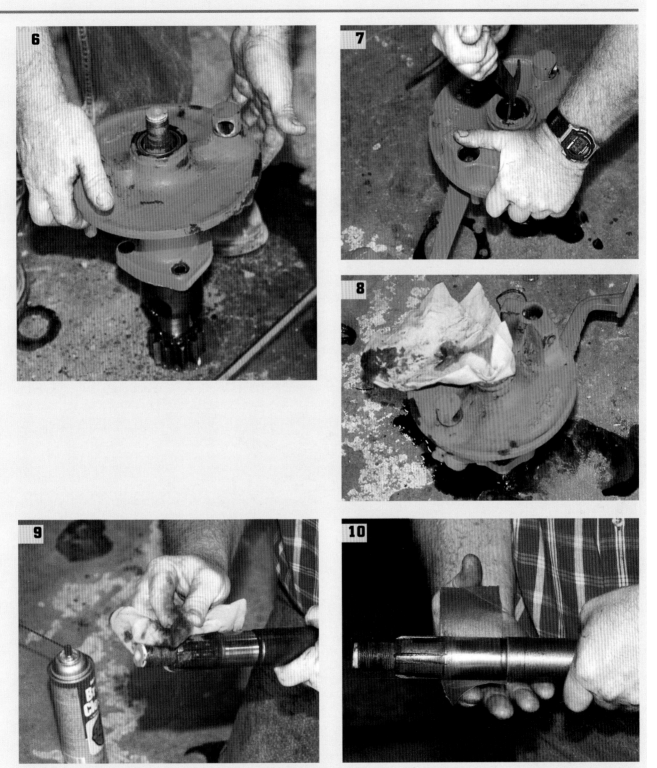

Renewal of the brake unit starts with replacing either or both of the brake shaft bushings and the oil seal. Bushings are typically in good shape, but the oil seal leaves a lot to be desired. Start by removing the seal with a seal remover (7); clean out the seal area well (8) and clean up the brake shaft (9). Inspect the area of the brake shaft that the seal rides on. You'll find grooves or a bit of corrosion or rust that will need cleaning up. To do this, dress the area of the brake shaft that the seal rides on with a piece of 320-grit emery paper (10). If the grooves are extensive or deep, you have no alternative other than to sleeve the shaft or find a replacement. Installing shaft sleeves is covered in the transmission chapter.

Transmission and Drivetrain Restoration

Installing a brake shaft seal, or any seal for that matter, requires just a little patience and care. The trick to driving them home is to make sure they start going perfectly square and true into the bore they rest in. In step 11 you can see the seal we will be driving. Get that seal straight and square to the bore and bring out a handy tool, a seal driver. I've used, and have seen, every round thing under the sun used as a seal driver; including sockets. If you can afford it, a seal driver makes this job a lot easier. In step 13, we drive it home using hard, but controlled, blows with an appropriately sized hammer. The first couple of hits should be light until you are sure the seal is driving home straight and true. After that, heavier blows from a heavier hammer will finish the job. Seal installation is complete by oiling the inside surface of the seal (14).

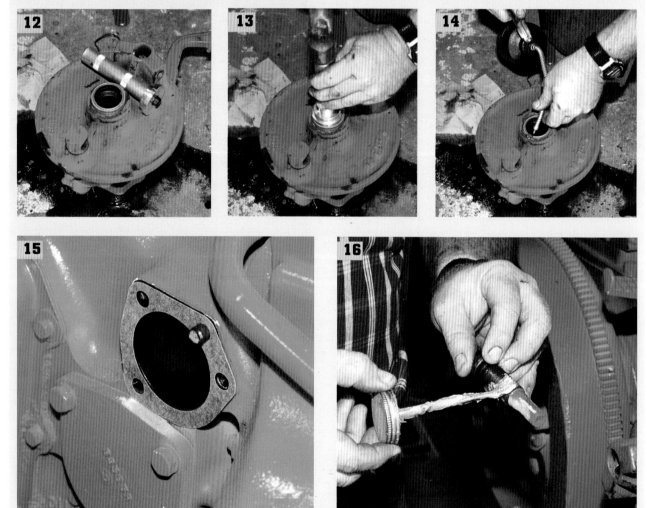

When installing the brake unit onto the tractor, use a new gasket. Gasket sealant is applied to the main case and the brake housing prior to installation.

After the entire brake unit is mounted on the tractor, start installing the rest of the braking system. Adjusting pins and screws should be coated with an anti-seizing compound. Brake pad rollers or pivot points should be lightly oiled. The remaining parts assemble in the reverse of removal.

SHIFTING MECHANISMS

The shifting mechanism is the component of the transmission that will show the most wear, and will be in the most need of restoration. The pivot point of the gearshift (the portion that rests and rotates in the shifter housing), the gate follower at the end of the gearshift, and the gates in the shift forks are all usually worn excessively. These parts will need to be replaced with better-quality used parts, or repaired. In addition, the shift forks are often bent slightly and should be straightened. Remember, these are cast parts that don't lend themselves well to bending, so use moderate and continuous pressure to straighten them. If they are bent severely, replace the entire fork. In addition, some models, notably the horizontal engine tractors with high-speed options, have secondary gates called "ears" that are typically broken and in need of repair (or have been repaired poorly in the past and need to be re-repaired). Other areas of the shift mechanism that need attention are the detent springs that help keep the transmission in each gear. These are often rusted or weak and need replacement. In short, a thorough restoration of the shifting mechanism will reward you with a machine that shifts so much more smoothly and quietly, you will hardly believe it. Take the time to do this well.

To restore the shifting mechanism, start with a complete disassembly. Remove the shift housing and cover plate from the tractor to expose the shift rails and shift forks. As mentioned earlier, the business end of the gearshift lever is almost guaranteed to be worn and in need of machining. Using a MIG welder, you can add material back to the end of the shifter; then file and grind the proper profile to the end. To add a perfect finishing touch, heat the end to red-hot and then let it slowly cool. This will soften the metal at the end of the gearshift back to a hardness that more closely matches the hardness of the shift fork. This process helps prevent excessive wear in the gates of the shift forks.

The forks can now be removed for repair by removing the shifter rails. The rails are locked in place with retaining screws on the left side of the maincase in horizontal engine tractors, the front in vertical engine tractors. To remove the forks, first remove the rails. To do this, remove the lock screws that hold the rails in place, remove the setscrews that retain the detent ball and spring, remove the spring, and then slide the rails out from the fork and transmission housing. On some tractors, the detent ball will come out of the fork when the rail is removed, so be ready to catch it as the rail clears each fork (on some tractors, the ball will stay in its bore).

Tips & Tricks

• Cleanliness is important when it comes to transmissions and drivetrains. The close tolerances in these systems will create wear and damage as dirt finds its way into them.

GEARSHIFT AND HOUSING

This is the gearshift and housing from a later Model B tractor. The gearshift should be inspected to see if any wear on the gate balls (the two nodules on the shaft) needs repair. The standard repair is to weld material on it, and then grind it back down to original dimensions. This gearshift is from a transmission with six speeds. Tractors with less than six forward speeds have a gearshift with only one gate ball at the end.

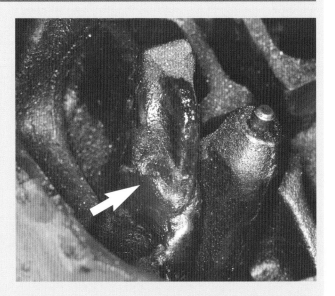

Pictured are the shift forks of a Model B tractor. The gates (passageways the gear shift moves in) are usually at least slightly worn, but if the gear shift gate nodules are welded and ground, then most of the "slop" created by wear will be removed through that repair. It is not uncommon to also find a fork ear that has been broken and repaired, as shown in the photograph above. This repair is clean and strong, but some are pretty poor and may need to be redone. The photograph directly below shows a lock plate on the right side of the tractor that the fork shafts mate to. It is tempting, but not necessary, to remove the shafts from this side after removal of this plate. Remove the setscrew on the left side of the tractor and pull the shafts out through the left side as shown in the photograph to the lower left. Disengage the detent balls and springs to remove. To do this, pull up the detent pin (shown in the above photograph about 3 o'clock to the repair) and insert a small cotter pin through a hole that will be exposed. This will remove tension and allow you to pull the shaft out easily through the right side of the main case. Some models of John Deere tractors don't have a detent disengage pinhole, and you have no choice but to remove the shaft without the aid of detent disengagement. To make matters worse, some detent balls, such as those found on the Model L, don't ride in countersunk bores, and when you remove the shaft, the balls will fall out of the forks. Be sure to be ready to catch these parts if needed.

Tips & Tricks

• Before working on the transmission, be sure to drain all fluids if you haven't already done so. Also, remember that the fluid capacities are quite large in the larger tractors, so have big containers ready to hold it all.

• Accurate, original restorations require painting a yellow primer inside the transmission cases of most models of John Deere tractors.

TRANSMISSION SHAFTS AND GEARS

The transmission of your John Deere tractor is simple but rugged, and requires simple, straightforward restoration procedures. Heavy-duty repairs, like cracked shafts, and housings, broken gears, or trashed bearings require parts replacement rather than repair. There is very little that was designed to be repaired or adjusted, or that was designed with frequent servicing or replacement in mind. If a part fails, it usually fails catastrophically. Therefore if disassembly reveals anything that is damaged, repairs to the part are usually out of the question and replacement is the only option. Unfortunately, this replacement can get expensive if you use new parts. It is cost-effective to think hard about the damage you have found, and weigh it against the tractor's intended use before committing to replacement of these parts with new instead of used parts in good condition.

For example, operators damage the teeth of second gear on almost all models of John Deere tractors. However, the damage is usually only to the front of the teeth and this damage represents no functional liability. This gear is certainly usable if you plan to only drive the tractor in a few shows and parades. However, if you also plan to do some work with the tractor and subject it to field loads, then you should probably replace it. Likewise, general gear wear in the transmissions of Dubuque-built tractors causes them to become noisy over the years. Unless this wear causes problems with gears skipping or the transmission jumping out of gear, then this wear doesn't represent a significant flaw. The tractor should be fine for continued light-duty use, especially if bearings are replaced to minimize the above-mentioned problems.

John Deere transmissions consist of gears, shafts, and bearings—nothing more, nothing less. What can make transmission restoration difficult is the precision, close tolerances, and heavy-duty nature of the transmission; nothing about the parts or procedures relating to one or a few of the models is unusual or overly complicated. The procedures to assemble, disassemble, and inspect these parts are common to all of the John Deere transmissions, and the operations, such as pulling bearings, are common to all of them as well. Therefore, rather than outline every gear, tooth, shim, or bolt, I'll continue with a couple of common service procedures for restoring transmissions. This will allow you to concentrate on the difficult steps without burdening you with detail of many different transmission models.

TRANSMISSION SHAFTS AND GEARS

With the gearshift forks and rails out of the way, we can concentrate on the transmission. Make a quick inspection of the gears and shafts. Shown in the first photograph are the sliding gears; the gears that move as you change gears. You may find gears that look like the one in the second photograph The teeth on the gear have leading edges that are chewed up (by the operators grinding the gears), but the gear is still strong, no teeth are cracked or missing, and the spline-ways through the center are not heavily worn. Replacing or repairing it would be ideal; reusing it is certainly acceptable.

Transmission and Drivetrain Restoration

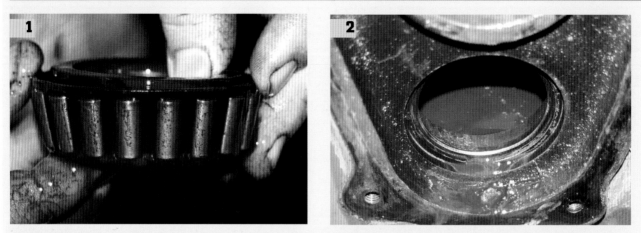

Most tractor transmissions—and John Deere tractors are no exceptions—accumulate moisture from condensation and outside storage. Because of this, most transmission bearings will show some signs of galling and corrosion. This left-side countershaft bearing and its mating cup show this clearly (2). Wear and corrosion will force us to replace these bearings.

On the transmission countershaft (the lower shaft), there is a roller assembly, shown here as two cages of long-needle bearings; that is the bearing on which the countershaft idler gear rotates. These roller assemblies are affordable and still available, and should be replaced unless they are still in excellent condition. The outboard, tapered, roller bearing at the right is typically past its useful life and will likely need replacement.

In the reduction gear cover, you'll see a bearing for the overdrive shaft, the shaft that the large reduction gear is mounted to. This bearing is easily driven on and off, if it needs replacement.

Photo 5 shows the high-speed sliding gear (lower gear), the high-speed gear fork, and the high-speed drive gear. Removal of these components is necessary to inspect and replace sliding gear-shaft bearings. Removal of the fork requires only the loosening of a set screw tied with mechanics wire), at which time the high-speed sliding gear will slide off the countershaft. After removing the cotter pin and nut that fastens the high-speed drive gear to the sliding gear shaft, the drive gear can be pulled. Photographs 6 and 7 outline the removal of the drive gear. Note that the setscrews holding the fork rails are visible. These are the three bolts near the top of photo 5 locked in place with mechanic's wire.

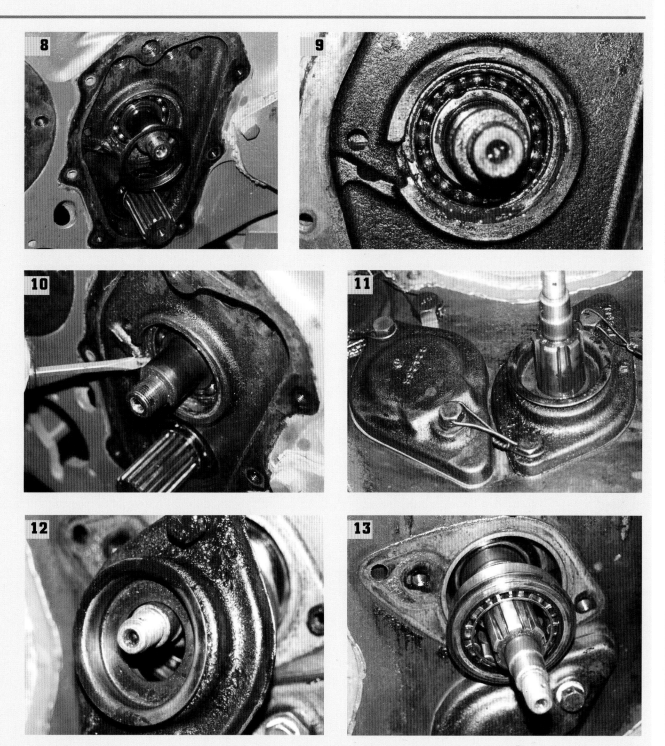

The sliding gear shaft, which looks like a continuous shaft from one side of the main case to the other, is actually a two-piece shaft coupled in the middle. The right side is the overdrive shaft and the left side is the sliding gear shaft. To remove the two shafts and bearings, remove the left side—sliding gear shaft—components first. Start with the retainer, shown resting on the shaft (8), and then the snap ring seen in steps 9 and 10. After taking off the snap ring, turn your attention to the right-hand side (11). Remove the overdrive shaft bearing cover (12). The bearing should come out easily (13), but a few light taps from a soft-faced mallet may be needed to get things started (14, next page). Work the two sides apart (15) and out (16). The last step is to inspect the bushing (17) inside the end of the overdrive shaft. This bushing may require replacement. Restoration is simply the replacement of any part that is damaged or doesn't meet your approval in wear or fit.

photos continued on next page

PULLING AND PRESSING BEARINGS (CONTINUED)

PULLING AND PRESSING BEARINGS

Restoration of the transmission will involve pulling and pressing various bearings from shafts and housings. Whereas some bearings, such as roller bearings, can be easy to remove, others, such as tapered roller bearings, usually require force to remove them. Removal requires the right tools and high-quality tools—no exceptions. The forces these tools are exposed to are tremendous; cheap tools are downright dangerous. Buy or rent high-quality pullers and presses. Next, I will cover the three common bearing removal/installation situations where removal procedures are the most difficult and require further explanation. These removal/installation methods for these situations can be adapted to other removal situations.

The first bearing removal procedure is the most difficult. In this case, a tapered roller bearing's cup is pressed into a housing that has no access, or limited access from the back of the cup. (All tapered roller bearings comprise two pieces; the bearing is called the cone, and the race it runs in is called the cup.) This can be a real bear, so be certain you need or want to replace the bearing before your start; you have only one choice if you want to remove the cup. Create three to four small spot welds with a MIG or stick welder on the inside surface of the cup; evenly space them around the circumference of the cup. This will

shrink the cup's circumference and allow the bearing to come out of its housing easily. The process destroys the cup, so reusing it isn't an option. If you want to reuse it, you can possibly shrink the cup enough to ease removal by packing it with dry ice. If you reuse the cup, you should also reuse the cone, if possible, because pairing a new cone with a worn cup may cause premature failure of the new cone.

In the second situation, the cone is pressed against the shoulder of a gear or the shaft. Getting the cone off requires the use of a bearing splitter, this is a device that will wedge itself between the cone and the shoulder. Once there, the splitter has tapped holes that can then be used to attach a bearing puller. In some circumstances it is safer for the operator and the part to use a shop press instead of attaching a puller to the splitter, to press off the bearing.

Tips & Tricks
• If you are not sure whether a bearing feels worn enough to replace, then it probably needs replacement. It is difficult to mistake a good bearing for a worn one, but it is possible for a worn bearing to feel somewhat OK or good enough.

SEALS AND SHAFTS

Repairing a shaft is required when there is rust damage, or wear from a seal has created a groove. To repair rust damage, the shaft must be sandblasted. If a smooth finish is required (hydraulic cylinder shaft) it also will have to be plated. Plating is fairly expensive; I recommend looking into a replacement shaft first. Plating is done with chrome or a chrome alloy. Because the customizations of many machines—such as Harley-Davidson motorcycles—involve chroming various parts, most customization shops can point you toward plating businesses in your area or region. Hydraulic-systems repair shops may be of assistance in locating plating shops, too.

There are several options for repairing significant grooves, but I recommend fitting a very thin sleeve over the groove. These sleeves are available, usually at bearing supply houses, in many sizes and are easy to install; I use Speedi-Sleeve. Insignificant gouges or minor grooves—grooves you can barely catch with a fingernail—can be filled with epoxy metal filler made for this purpose (also available at bearing supply houses) and sanded flush with 600-grit or finer emery paper. This is made easier if you can chuck the shaft into some kind of slow-spinning lathe or drill. Then use a wet strip of emery paper, held under the shaft as a sling, and let the spinning of the shaft do the work. Otherwise, you can rotate the shaft with one hand while you hold the emery paper around the shaft with the other.

REMOVING THE COUNTERSHAFT

To remove the countershaft, remove the bearing cover on the right side of the main case (top left). Note that the bearing preload on this shaft is adjusted through the use of shims under this cover—keep these shims. Then, remove the locking retainer on the right side (top right). Keeping the shaft still while you try to loosen this retainer may require a block of wood placed against one of the gears on the shaft. This nut requires either a hub socket, similar to one used to remove four-wheel-drive truck spindle nuts, or a punch and a hammer to get it started. The second photograph shows it off the threads, resting on the shaft. At this time a little driving force from the left side (lower left) will drive the countershaft out through the gears on the shaft and out the right side of the main case (lower right).

Transmission and Drivetrain Restoration

PTO

There are two primary subassemblies in John Deere PTO (power take-off) systems that need attention during a restoration: the seal at the back of the tractor and the bearings in which the shaft runs. Removal of the PTO assembly depends on the model, but there are two general designs that are used. The first is the transmission countershaft design that you will find on Dubuque model tractors, and on the more traditional takeoff shaft design used by the horizontal-engine models. The countershaft design means that the PTO shaft is nothing more than an extended transmission shaft that extends all the way to the rear of the tractor. In the traditional takeoff design, the power take-off shaft is separate from the transmission countershaft. This shaft is driven through the use of mated bevel gears driven by the transmission sliding gear shaft.

Using the manuals, you shouldn't have too much problem removing the assemblies, but keep in mind a couple of things. The gaskets under one or more of the seal or bearing covers (which cover depends on the model; you'll be able to discern during disassembly) act as shims that adjust bearing preload and gear lash.

Noting and keeping all of the gaskets to reuse, or to use as guides during reassembly, is important. During reassembly, add or delete gaskets to maintain the proper preload force on the shaft bearings and gear lash. The manuals are usually vague on the proper preload and lash specification, so you'll have to reassemble the PTO using "feel" to adequately set these specs. Preload and lash is correct when you can spin the PTO shaft without feeling any binding, grinding, or chattering, yet there should be very little if any rotation of the shaft that is free or loose. If you can't remove the free play and looseness without creating a grinding or binding sensation, then the gearing is heavily worn and should be replaced. If replacement of the gearing isn't an option, then err on the side of slight looseness. This looseness may slightly accelerate wear, but excessive tightness may damage or break the associated gearing and shafts.

Tips & Tricks

• Be sure to use mechanics' wire to lock all fasteners that call for it when reassembling the transmission.

BELT PULLEY

The belt pulley will need attention during restoration. The lubrication design of the crankshaft-driven belt pulleys of the Waterloo tractors clearly did not anticipate that the belt pulley would spend much time free running, that is, the belt pulley turning or crankshaft turning with the engine clutch disengaged. Considering the age of these tractors, you'll usually find that free running has occurred enough times to create significant wear in the belt-pulley bearings and/or bushings (some have just one type, others have both). I recommend closely inspecting these items to determine if they need replacing. Some bearings or bushings have been replaced in the recent past and may be OK to reuse, but be sure to check. Smooth, problem-free operation of the clutch depends on a smooth-running belt pulley.

I normally replace the belt-pulley cover clips as a matter of course unless these items are already in excellent shape. Drilling out the rivets will remove the clips. Because the rivets come all the way through to the outside of the belt pulley, doing an excellent job of riveting

is important for cosmetic and safety reasons if you plan to use your tractor on belt load (improperly riveted clips can leave exposed rivet heads that can tear and break belts). Hire this work out if you are not comfortable with your own riveting skills. The clutch components of the Waterloo tractor belt pulleys are covered in the clutch section of chapter 3.

The belt pulleys of vertical-engine tractors are entirely different. The pulleys are paper-type pulleys, the restoration of which is best left to specialty repair shops, found in the appendices. The associated gearing requires full disassembly, inspection, and careful reassembly. The belt-pulley shaft runs in tapered roller bearings that will probably need to be replaced. The shaft is driven by a pair of bevel gears found on the end of the shaft and on the PTO shaft. As found with the PTO shaft, the seal cover gaskets act as shims to provide bearing preload and gear lash. Careful reassembly will be required to arrive at a gasket combination that provides the proper lash and preload. You should replace the seal with every restoration.

Restoring the auxiliary power systems of a tractor is more than just replacing a few leaky seals. All systems should be disassembled and inspected; parts should be replaced or renewed as necessary; the systems must be reassembled; and all adjustments must be made. The tractor in these photographs is a John Deere Model 60. The systems on the Model 60 have several updated features such as a clutch-based, live PTO, and a draft-sensing hydraulic system, yet, it retains most of the same design style and sensibilities of the earliest hydraulic lift and PTO systems on the letter-series tractors.

Here are homemade remote hydraulic ports added to a Model G. This on-site enhancement is fairly common.

This is a close-up of the PTO reduction gear and PTO shaft bearing. The gear will show some wear. Any light wear found is acceptable, but gear teeth that are broken or show excessive wear or corrosion should be replaced. The bearing may or may not need to be replaced depending on the amount of time the tractor spent on PTO work.

This is a close-up of the PTO-driven shaft, and the gear and replacement bearing for this shaft. Once again, bearing replacement is not mandatory, depending on the number of hours the tractor spent on a PTO load. Each bearing should be inspected on a case-by-case basis.

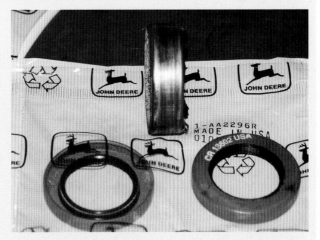

The original PTO shaft seal, shown on end, is quite thick and contains a dust felt to keep dirt out. The authorized John Deere replacements are thin and have no dust seal. Installing only one seal is acceptable, but a better strategy is to install two seals. Both are driven into the housing. The inner seal has the lip facing the interior of the transmission housing, thereby keeping oil in. The outer seal is installed with the lip facing toward the outside. This will help keep dust and dirt out.

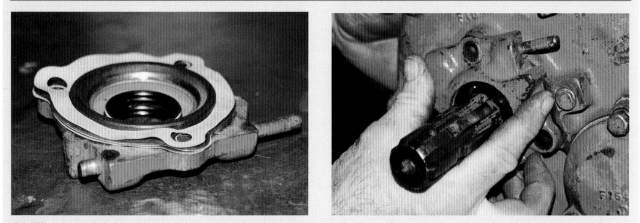

The PTO seal cover also adjusts the preload of the shaft bearings. Adjusting this preload requires adding and deleting shims and gaskets from the cover (shown right), until the bearing preload is properly set.

HYDRAULICS

There are three primary subsystems on any hydraulic system. They are the pump, the control valve, and the cylinder. The pump is responsible for providing the hydraulic pressure, the control valve assembly accepts operator input and directs pressure in response to that input, and the cylinder actually does the work of raising and lowering the implement attached to the hydraulic system. The first and the last subsystems are within the grasp of any weekend mechanic. The pumps on most John Deere Two-Cylinder tractors are simple, and are of the gear-driven type, much like oil pumps. Cylinder designs likewise are simple, and are simply a housing in which one or more pistons with an attached rod accept incoming pressure to move the attached implement up and down or rotate an attached rocker shaft.

The control valve is another matter. These units are composed of parts that require very close tolerances and fit to operate correctly. In addition, complete testing of most of the John Deere hydraulic control-valve subsystems requires advanced understanding and expensive specialty tools. For these reasons, restoring the assemblies yourself is not advised unless you are willing to take the time to do further research on general hydraulic system repair and adjustment. To help you on your way and augment your further research, I'll cover the restoration of the John Deere model 60 hydraulic control-valve assembly in the photos. This subassembly is identical to the hydraulic control subassemblies found on most of the later letter series and most number series Deere tractors.

PUMPS

Before starting pump removal, check on the availability of NOS hydraulic pump parts. Occasionally, complete rebuild kits can be found that will have everything you need—if you find one you can afford. To restore hydraulic pumps, start by removing and plugging the hydraulic lines and plugging the ports in the pump. The pumps are mounted to and driven by the governor (horizontal-engine tractors) or mounted to the front of the engine and driven by the camshaft (vertical-engine tractors). Remove the pump in its entirety.

Once off the tractor, restoring the pump is like restoring any gear-driven pump, such as the engine's oil pump. Start disassembly by removing the pump cover from the pump body. Be careful to preserve as much of the gasket found between these two parts as possible. This cover-to-body pump gasket also serves as a shim, and you'll need to use it as a guide to choose gasket material, and as an outline when you cut a new gasket. At this point, you'll be able to see the two pump gears that provide the pressure for the hydraulic system. Usually all bushings, and both gears, will need to be replaced. To check the bushings, look for any looseness or excessive clearance. The gears and shafts should be a slip fit; that is, they should spin easily, but with no discernible play. Visually inspect the gears; excessive wear can sometimes be seen with a quick inspection. If the gears look OK, check the clearance between the pump gears and the body with a feeler gauge; the manual for your tractor will have this dimension. Failure

to pass a visual or clearance measurement indicates the need for replacement.

In the pump body, around the shaft driven by the engine, you will find a seal that keeps the hydraulic fluid from leaving the pump body and dumping into the engine. If the seal leaks, hydraulic fluid will be lost to the engine. This seal typically needs to be replaced. When replacing this seal, carefully inspect the shaft for any type of noticeable groove, then sleeve the shaft if a groove is found. Because of the pressure involved, any type of groove in the shaft will allow a leak, even with a new seal.

RESTORING A PTO CLUTCH

Pictured is a Model 60 PTO clutch fork. Typically, the fork-related parts are in fine shape and can be reused with one exception: The copper clutch fork shoes that contact the clutch pack should be checked to see if they are worn enough to merit replacement.

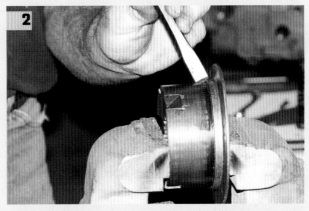

The clutch cam disc has to be punched to prevent the disc from spinning on the clutch cam. Gary Uken, of Uken Restorations, uses a cold chisel and a hammer to set this punch.

A punch and hammer is required to remove the clutch cam disc from the clutch cam. The disc is also punch set; be sure to bend back any punches seen before you try to drive this off.

Clutch pack springs are a bit of a bear to get in place. The easiest way is to simply line them up on the hardened washer. Don't forget the three, smaller inner springs (5).

continued on next page

Transmission and Drivetrain Restoration

Above: The clutch cam, with disc installed, is then placed on the springs.

Next, place the clutch brake plate on the cam disc. The placements of the holes in the housing that mounts the stationary components of the clutch pack, such as this brake plate, are not symmetrical. Note the orientation of the brake plate. Be sure the plate holes and the housing holes line up (8).

Below and below right: Anchor the clutch brake plate with three fasteners—final tightening or locking is not necessary, they will be loosened later for clutch adjustment—then install the clutch collar. Before installing the collar, install the collar pin, which is a small, square-shouldered pin (9). This will fit in a mated groove in the clutch cam. Place the balls on the cam to finish the collar installation (10).

The clutch-adjusting cam hub is slipped down onto the shaft first; be sure to install the small spring. The clutch-adjusting cam is tightened down against the collar and a setscrew (11) is placed in the hub through one of the openings in the clutch-adjusting cam. The adjusting cam adjusts the disengagement pressure of the clutch pack, but the amount of tightening is unimportant at this point. We can't adjust the clutch until it is all put back together. Simply tighten the clutch-adjusting cam just enough so that the top of it is below the top of the clutch-adjusting cam hub.

Please note that the oil passageway hole in the shaft must line up with the circular cutouts found on the clutch-lined discs.

Begin creating the clutch pack by starting with a lined clutch faceplate, then a lined disc, alternating lined and drive discs until you finish. End the stack with the other lined clutch faceplate. Be sure to alternate hard surface discs and lined discs throughout the stack.

Transmission and Drivetrain Restoration

This picture contrasts new and old clutch discs. The one on the right is burnt and worn thin; interestingly, the lining is offset. There was no evidence that the lining had wandered after installation. More than likely, the lining was improperly bonded to the disc when new.

After the clutch drive and lined discs are installed, three springs must be installed down through the cutouts found in the lined discs.

Using a spare clutch drum from a salvage tractor (or the one you removed from the tractor), line up the clutch discs. Withdraw the drum slowly to maintain alignment.

Install the clutch-pack snap ring and bushing/thrust washer (not shown, and changed during the production run of the tractors).

Above: With the snap ring in place, engage the clutch. Do this with two pry bars after you have reinstalled the clutch drum/aligning tool to maintain alignment of the clutch discs. It should take a lot of force to engage the clutch. Remove the drum/alignment tool (20). Photograph 21 illustrates the gap created between the clutch collar and brake plate when the clutch is engaged. The clutch is engaged properly when a definite, distinct snap is felt. A clutch that requires only minimal force to engage or exhibits a reluctance to engage indicates that further adjustment needs to be performed. To adjust the clutch, disengage it, remove the setscrew from the collar, and turn the adjusting collar so the collar moves upward to increase the amount of force required to engage the clutch or turn the collar downward to do the opposite. After the clutch is installed on the tractor, more adjustment may be necessary to create clutch action that feels distinct, sure and strong. Some manuals provide specifications of engagement force. Regardless of the tractor, adjusting it by feel alone is adequate, especially if you have operated these tractors before and you are familiar with how they operate and feel.

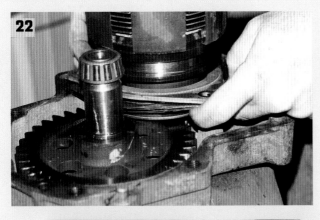

Left and below: The brake plate must be shimmed for proper operation (22). When the brake plate was installed, we returned the same shims that were removed during disassembly as a starting point. To see if these shims will do the trick, measure the clearance between the brake plate and the clutch cam disc (23). The clearance specifications for this Model 60 are .090 inch, but check your service manual for your particular tractor. Simply add or remove shims as necessary to obtain this clearance. Don't forget to bend up the corners of the brake-plate mounting-bolt locking tabs (24).

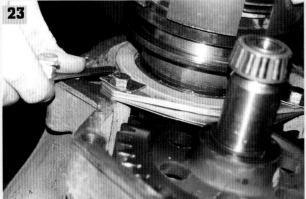

LIFTS AND CYLINDERS

As external parts, some wear is acceptable on lift arms and linkages, and restoration isn't really necessary except when wear is excessive. New parts are not available so your only choice is to replace your parts with used parts. Just be careful to inspect used components, since most are no better than those you are replacing. I don't recommend purchasing them unless you can inspect them, or can return them if they are not in as good condition as the ones you are replacing. If your lift is collectible—and therefore valuable, as is the 801 lift—then a better-quality used lift will not be available unless you have deep pockets. The best option here is to find a local machine shop that can restore the linkage. Most parts of the lift that are worn can have material added through welding. This material is then machined back to specification to look and act like new. The machine shop also can repair any cracks or previous repairs that are of poor quality. Assembly of the lift arms follows disassembly. Just be sure to use new keys (the half-moon pieces of metal that fix the lift arms' position on the rocker-arm shaft). Care should be taken that the arms are completely immobile on the shafts.

The power to lift the implement comes from pressure that builds in a hydraulic ram that is internal to the tractor. This ram in turn pushes on an arm that rotates the lift shaft. A full restoration includes pulling the hydraulic ram and piston and fully inspecting it. The packing and seals should be replaced if the parts are available, and the shaft will have to be plated if it has corroded and pitted. Installing new seals and packing around a shaft that is pitted will cause erosion of the seal, resulting in leaks. The bore the piston rides in inside the cylinder may also be pitted or scored. This bore can be machined to return it to its original smooth and unblemished finish. At that time, depending on how much material had to be removed from the bore to arrive at this finish, an oversized piston should be made or found, or a new wider and thicker piston sealing ring can be found to accommodate the larger bore diameter. Parts for the hydraulic system in general, and the ram in particular, are difficult to find. The NOS dealers listed in the appendices can be of help, as can modern hydraulic repair shops.

Although transmission and power system restoration is not easy and quick, it is simple if you take the time to be thorough and inspect everything completely, being sure to replace or repair anything that is amiss. If you get stuck or frustrated with your particular tractor, remember that many of the parts suppliers in the appendices are very knowledgeable and can help steer you in the right direction. Of course they are not in the business of providing free advice, but a quick call or two with a question that results in a parts order will be welcomed. If you reach the point where you need professional help to continue with the project, there are several excellent restoration shops mentioned in the appendices that will perform part of the restoration. I feel certain that you can do the work yourself, though, if you are patient, study this book and your manuals, and complete your research through a conversation with an experienced restorer. There is nothing here that a mechanically inclined person can't do.

THE HYDRAULIC CONTROL ASSEMBLY

Many of the plugs found in the hydraulic control assembly have shims, backing rings, or washers to watch for as you remove the plug. This plug backs the pressure-relief spring.

Removing the check valve assembly is much easier with a magnetic pickup tool. Here, the tool has just extracted the check valve itself.

This is a collection of the parts removed from the Powr-Trol operating valve. There really aren't that many, and the concept behind the system isn't difficult. What is important is the precise tolerance of the parts required to maintain and control high system pressures. Any corrosion found on the parts returned to the control system, or any dirt in the system, will most likely lead to system failure.

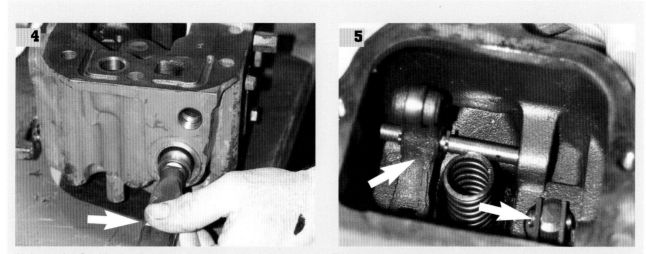

In photograph 4, Gary Uken installs the operating valve; proper orientation is shown. The operating valve of the tractor will have a specific orientation; note it from the service manual or from your disassembly notes. In photograph 5 you can see the control arm installed, to the right, with a small rivet and two small metal plates hanging to its sides, and the cam latch arm, to the left with a roller, and the cam follower spring. These parts must be installed before the cam follower and cam holder.

Seen here is the cam holder ready for installation. The centering cam and the cam blades have not been removed from the cam holder, but the two screws holding them in will be loosened later to adjust hydraulic lift lever free play and the locking behavior of the lift lever. These blades will ride on the roller seen on the cam follower arm (slightly below center in the photograph).

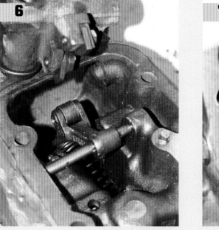

Installing the cam holder requires some strength. The cam-follower arm spring is pretty stout, and you'll need to hold the cam holder down while you install the cam lever rockshaft; an extra set of hands helps.

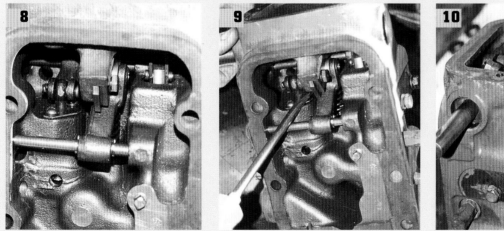

To install the cam holder and lift-lever rockshaft, first install a woodruff key in the middle of the lift-lever shaft. Install the lift lever by installing it though the housing hole and then through the cam holder. Since the cam holder assembly has to pressed down against a spring while the lift lever is installed through it, an extra set of hands may be helpful.

Here is the rockshaft installed. The dust seals can be installed later in the recessed openings in the housing around the rockshaft.

THE HYDRAULIC CONTROL ASSEMBLY (CONTINUED)

Inspect the check valve and relief valve assemblies for replacement, or clean parts. Begin installation of the check valves by dropping the first ball into the check valve bore. Then drop the check valve into the hole. Shown is the metering check valve during assembly. A magnetic pickup tool is real handy for this work during disassembly and assembly.

Next, drop in the check valve (12).

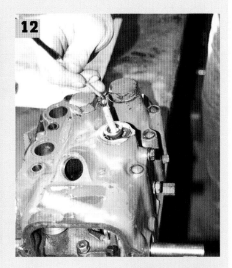
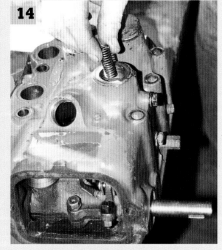

The second check-valve ball goes in next.

The check-valve spring is dropped in last and the check-valve hole is plugged up (14). Don't forget the washer that goes on the check-valve plug.

Here are the throttle valve and spring and, at the bottom of the housing, the adjusting screw for this throttle valve (15). This adjusting screw, and a second adjusting screw on the left side of the housing (16) adjust the hydraulic system pressures and drop rates. Your service manual has the specifics on hydraulic system adjustments.

The last step in restoring the control valve is bolting it up to the rear cover (17). Use a new gasket and plenty of sealant when doing this.

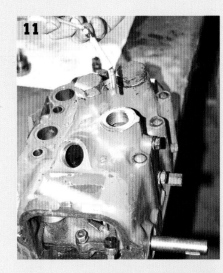

When you first buy your tractor, it's likely that pipe plugs from a plumbing supply shop are used as hydraulic remote port plugs. If originality is your goal, you'll need to add more authentic port plugs, such as the ones shown here. The one on the right is for a number-series tractor, the one on the left is for an older letter series. These are not interchangeable, so be careful to find the right one for your tractor when purchasing used outlet port plugs at a salvage yard.

Right: Here is the business end of a hydraulic lift. The hydraulic ram, hidden behind the dark ram arm, drives the ram arm out and in. This ram arm is attached to the rockshaft, which the lift linkage arms are attached to. As the hydraulic ram is pushed out by hydraulic pressure, or drawn in from the lack of pressure, the ram arm is pushed in or out rotating the rockshaft in the process. This rotation lifts or lowers the lift linkage arms, raising or lowering the implement.

An Out-of-the-Way but Strong and Stable Jack Stand Crossbeam

Finding a solid, flat area to place a jack stand to support your tractor can sometimes be a problem. It is especially important when you start banging and heaving on wheels, axles, and other components—actions that could cause the tractor to slip off the jack stands. A really handy device used with jack stands to support the tractor can be easily made from a heavy piece of bar stock. I recommend bar stock that is 1 inch thick by 2 inches wide as the minimum for smaller tractors. A steel supplier can help you with the size needed for larger tractors. The length should be at least 2-1/2 feet wider than the width of the transmission case.

To attach the bar stock device, start by removing the drawbar/draw hitch frame from the tractor. Using the draw-hitch frame as a guide, drill two holes in the bar stock that match up with two holes in the drawbar frame. Then bolt the steel bar to the underside of the tractor where the hitch frame was located. After lifting the tractor, place two jack stands, one at each end of the bar stock as close as possible to the tractor, then lower the tractor. This is a great support because it's stable, out of the way, makes it highly unlikely the tractor will slide off the stands, and covers very little of the bottom of the transmission case, allowing for easy access during painting.

chapter 6

Cosmetic Restoration

"One thing the inventors can't seem to get the bugs out of is fresh paint."
—*Unknown*

The start of cosmetic restoration signifies a turning point in a restoration. By now you have completed most of the tedious and dirty disassembly work, and most if not all of the mechanical restoration. As your tractor sits partially reassembled, ready for bodywork and paint, it's easy to visualize the tractor completed, resplendent in its new paint and ready to use, show, and enjoy. Getting the tractor from its current condition to one where it's ready for paint is what this chapter will help you do. This is the homestretch of the restoration.

SURFACE PREPARATION

The first step in cosmetic restoration is preparation of the surfaces to receive coatings and paint. This preparation includes initial cleaning of the surfaces, straightening and fitting all sheet metal, last-minute parts repair and replacement, and a final cleaning. During this phase you'll also separate the cosmetic restoration tasks into manageable sizes. Moving ahead with a plan is particularly important during cosmetic work, because as soon as you start cleaning a piece of sheet metal, you are committing to completing the entire restoration sequence for that piece within a limited amount of time. Cleaning starts a chain of events that is continually driven onward by the risk of rust and by coat/recoat times of the painting system you'll be using.

Cleaning leaves the metal bare, and the process of rust begins immediately after the surface is exposed. As soon as you complete your repairs and clean the metal, you will have to apply primer to the metal to protect it from rust. Most primers require that you start applying filler coats and/or topcoats within a few days. Whereas some filler coats effectively seal the metal and prevent rust, the chemical make-up of these fillers requires applying the final paint (called the color coat) within a certain period of time. Breaking the task of cosmetic restoration into small chores is important for a good-looking restoration and a top-quality finish.

CLEANING

Some cleaning has to be done before repairs can begin. There is no need to completely clean any particular part right now; it's sufficient to clean or sandblast just those areas that need to be repaired. After the repairs and fitting, you can apply these methods to completely clean a part or panel in preparation for coats of primer and paint. We covered all of the different methods for paint stripping earlier in the book, and by now you have enough experience to judge for yourself which method you'll use for each of the remaining pieces that need work. Because surface preparation dictates the final quality of the cosmetic restoration, you'll want to spend adequate time cleaning and prepping the sheet-metal surfaces for paint.

WELDING

Welding skills, equipment, and techniques are required for the patching and straightening phase. Welding during sheet-metal repair takes on three forms: installation of patch panels, repairing cracks and tears, and heating. Although these tasks can be accomplished with a gas-welding outfit, repairs with a gas torch require a deft hand, experience, and extremely good equipment. Most amateur welders prefer to heat with a gas-welding outfit, and repair with what is commonly referred to as a MIG outfit (gas metal arc welding, GMAW, is more accurate). Stick welding (shielded metal arc welding, SMAW) has no real place in cosmetic restoration because stick welding sheet metal without burning holes is nearly impossible for the nonprofessional. You'll want some training before striking your first arc with your new welding outfit. The welders' supply house that sells you your equipment likely will provide training for free or at a nominal cost.

Tips & Tricks

• Training for some of the skills and techniques needed for bodywork is available at your local community college.

Removing Spot Welds

If two pieces of metal are spot-welded together and you need to separate them, the spot weld will have to be drilled out. To find the spot welds, use a wire wheel to remove rust and paint from those areas you deem likely to have a spot weld. If that doesn't reveal them, heavy liquid dye, like Rit dye, applied to these areas may expose the minute heat and stress cracks usually present on spot welds. Drill out each weld with a 7/16-inch bit that has a flat tip with a pilot burr. When reattaching, the holes made by the bit and the small pilot hole made by the flat tip bit's burr will help you align the pieces.

Sheet-Metal Myth

You'll hear many people repeat the advice that you should never sandblast sheet metal because the heat from the process warps the metal. This is true for thinner sheet metal commonly found in equipment made within the last 20 to 30 years, but these old tractors have substantial sheet metal—usually 18-gauge and better—that stands up to sandblasting much better. Even so, there are a few caveats and considerations. You definitely don't want to use a huge, high-volume industrial sandblasting machine to sandblast your sheet metal; this equipment would indeed warp the metal. A siphon-style blaster or a home shop-sized pressure blaster will be gentle enough for your tractor's sheet metal if you keep the pressure down to 75-90 psi.

Just remember that with either method, you must keep the sandblaster's gun moving and never sandblast any one spot for too long. Be especially careful around heavily rusted areas and where the sheet metal is thinner, such as tight curves and corners that may be thin enough to warp under the small amounts of heat your sandblaster can generate. If you are still concerned after considering these issues, a switch in blasting media may be the ticket. Other blasting media, such as soda or crushed nutshells (usually walnut; pecans in the South), will do the work with less heat. If you decide that sandblasting a particular piece is out of the question, just remember that other abrasive methods, such as a wire wheel, also generate heat, and the same precautions should be taken.

Tips & Tricks

• When hammering out large, shallow dents, backing the metal with sandbags or bags of lead shot is easier and quicker than backing it with a dolly.

• Cleanliness is next to godliness when prepping metal for paint. Remove every trace of rust before moving on to the painting steps.

STRAIGHTENING

Straightening dents is easy, right? Just back the metal with a body dolly or sandbag, and beat it within an inch of its life. Unfortunately, it's harder than that. Understanding the process requires that you keep the following thought in mind. Sheet metal that has been bent or dented has been stretched to some extent. This means that dents, bends, and tears will deform metal to the point that its surface area, in the vicinity of the dent, is larger than it used to be. Simply beating it straight may leave a surface that will be dimpled or wavy. For example, if you take a piece of aluminum foil, cut it into a perfect square, and then crumple it, all the straightening in the world won't return it to its original size, and it will no longer be true and square. The same thing happens with sheet metal. When manual straightening doesn't yield an acceptable surface, you have three choices based on the severity of the flawed surface.

"Shrinking" the sheet metal may repair minor and moderate imperfections. In essence, this process reduces the extra surface area of the metal created by the stretching action of the original dent. After shrinking, you should have a reasonably smooth surface that may need little or no body filler or sanding to correct to a final finish.

Two methods exist for shrinking metal. The first is to use specialized body hammers when hammering out the dent. Body picks, swirling hammers, and similar hammers will shrink the metal by "gathering" the metal, and reducing the surface area of the dent.

To help you visualize this, let's say you have a 12x12-inch piece of foil, but it needs to fit inside an 11-1/2x 11-1/2-inch frame. To make it fit, you crumple the aluminum foil on purpose and straighten it with your fingers. As I mentioned before, crumpling reduces the surface area of the foil. Once you do this a few times, the foil will eventually lay reasonably flat and square inside the frame. That is what these specialized body hammers do: they crumple the metal in the area of the dent as you beat the dent, reducing the surface area of the metal by gathering it into very small swirls, dimples, and undulations. The surface is then smooth enough that you can eliminate any roughness with a small amount of body filler. This method has great success with some moderate dents, but only limited success with more severe dents.

The second method of shrinking metal is called heat shrinking. Heat shrinking involves heating the affected

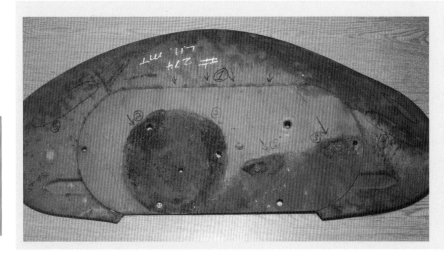

This fender shows all the typical problems associated with sheet metal: In-seam rust (1), heavy surface rust (2), rust perforations (3), bents and dents that stretch the metal (4), and shallow depression dents (5). Repairing this is a challenge, but not impossible to accomplish for a weekend restorer.

area until it is red-hot, then quenching it with water. This rapid cooling causes the crystals of metal to join more closely, and thereby shrink the metal. This may be done in several passes around the area of the dent to obtain the surface you need. This process also hardens the metal, so you may have difficulty working the dent with manual methods afterward. The metal also may crack if it is worked excessively or dented again. Heat shrinking is usually used in conjunction with manual straightening.

A third strategy used to shrink metal is to create a set of strategically placed drill holes (3/16-inch to 1/4-inch seem to work well) and saw kerfs with a handheld drill and a jigsaw. This method removes metal to create free space into which the straightened metal can move. When followed by heat shrinking, this can create a very nice surface. The holes and kerfs can then be filled using a MIG welder and ground smooth with a grinder afterward. The optimum location for the holes and kerfs depends entirely on the geometry of the dent. Typically, you will drill a hole in the center of the dent and saw three to six radial lines from this point until the blade reaches an undamaged area. If the damage is more of a crease, drilling a hole in the deepest part and then sawing a kerf along the axis of the crease is usually best. If the surface is more of a rumple, or if it's an area that has been straightened in the past and only dimples and waves exist, then careful examination of the surface should reveal the best places to drill holes.

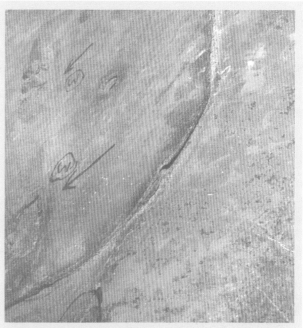

When assessing sheet metal, look between affixed panels. Here, rust has worked its way between the fender brace panel and the fender it's attached to. This will require extensive work to take apart so that the rust can be removed.

Tips & Tricks

• Tractor sheet metal is typically stout enough to sandblast, and sandblasting sheet metal is the most efficient way to prepare the surface for repairs and painting.

Judgment Calls: Deciding When to Replace or Repair

One of the most difficult parts of bodywork is the period of time when you first inventory all of the problems in the sheet metal on your tractor. It's easy to become overwhelmed at this point with the scope of work, its potential costs, and the prospect of tackling projects with which you have little or no experience. When you reach this point, it's helpful to ask whether the flaw will require welding equipment to repair. If you don't know, try straightening or repairing it with hand tools first. You'll realize quickly if the piece requires heat or patching—two things that require welding equipment. At that point you'll have two groups of flaws: those that require only hand tools and those that will need welding equipment or professional attention. Body tools are relatively inexpensive, so simple dents and dings can and should be repaired by you. There is no magic or difficult skill involved in hammering out dents if you are careful and pay attention to how the metal is behaving.

Severe flaws in the sheet metal that require welding equipment to repair need additional thought. Welding equipment is expensive and its purchase can be tough to justify. If the sheet metal on your tractor requires a lot of welding repairs and you're willing to try it on your own, it will help to remember that welding equipment is less expensive than buying just two or three replacement pieces of sheet metal. If you aren't willing to try welding repairs on your own, and the estimates you are getting from the professionals send you reeling, then try "trading up." Used replacement sheet metal with rust and light dents and dings can be purchased very inexpensively. For very little money, you can trade up to a piece of sheet metal you can fix with hand tools.

PATCHING

Severely damaged areas or heavily rusted surfaces will require removal and replacement with a new and straight piece of metal. This process is known as patching. To do this, first mark off the damaged area and then drill a hole at a corner of your outline to start a jigsaw cut. Cut out the area, and use the opening to trace a pattern onto poster board. Use the pattern to transfer the outline to the replacement piece of sheet metal. After cutting out the replacement piece with the jigsaw, check the fit and make any necessary adjustments to its outline with a small grinder or the saw. Place this patch piece into the opening in the sheet metal and hold it in place with tape or magnets. Using the MIG welder, place a few spot welds around the circumference of the patch. Now that these welds are holding the new patch piece in place, remove the tape or magnets and place a generous number of additional spot welds around the circumference until the patch is in place securely. Grind the welds smooth, fill the areas between the welds with body filler, sand smooth, and you're done! Of course, this process is much harder than I let on, especially if you are new to welding. Just remember that care and patience will go a long way toward creating an excellent and unnoticeable (after the paint is applied) patch repair.

Restoring the sheet metal of your tractor will invariably require the replacement of sections of metal. This section (seen here above the hole) had become perforated with rust holes. Removal exposes underlying structural metal that is also heavily rusted. Gary Uken of Uken Restorations will remove all rust from the underlying metal and weld a replacement patch in place. **Gary Uken**

DIFFICULT REPAIRS

Many times you will be presented with a difficult circumstance. For instance, the edges of many pieces of sheet metal are rolled tightly to present a smooth and finished edge. This rolled edge is known as a wire roll, because the roll actually contains a piece of wire inside. If a section of wire roll needs to be replaced, you are faced with a dilemma. This process is impossible to duplicate in a home shop, so a local sheet-metal fabrication shop will have to create it for you. This is often prohibitively expensive, even if you can find a shop that will do the work. If the wire rolling is damaged beyond the point that you can repair it yourself, you should check with a few metal fabrication shops in your area and see if they can repair it for a reasonable fee. If not, replacing the entire panel may be necessary.

Flanging is the process of creating a seam of bent metal. There are flanging tools you can use to recreate it. Simple step flanges are best created with a tool called, appropriately enough, a flanging tool. If you must recreate a specialized flange or other profile for which there isn't a tool, you can often, with a little resourcefulness and patience, create the tools you need yourself. When I repair sheet metal that requires a special shape or profile, I first create an anvil in the profile I need, shaped out of bar steel or hard wood. Then I gently work the sheet metal around and onto this anvil with a small body or ball-peen hammer. With patience and a careful eye I can often get excellent results—a little creativity goes a long way.

An anvil also works well when you need to straighten grille bars. The bars on the grilles of most John Deere tractors have a shallow U-shape profile to them. I simply shape a small section of steel or hard wood in the profile I need, then I use it as backing when I hammer the bar straight. The anvil usually has to be mounted on something substantial, like a regular blacksmith anvil, vise, or a heavy workbench. Heat shrinking used in conjunction with this procedure works with grille bars. Most of the other corners, flares, and shapes you'll see in John Deere sheet metal can be straightened with standard body dollies. If not, shaping extra steel or wood to use as a dolly will help you get the curve and form you need for a good-looking piece of sheet metal.

There are many other circumstances you'll run across that will create unique challenges. One example is a dented gas tank. This may not be a problem if you have a styled tractor, because the hood often hides the gas tank. Dented tanks on unstyled tractors usually have to be fixed and are a difficult problem to solve. Safety dictates that you want a fuel tank that holds fuel forever without any risk. Trying to repair a tank that is damaged in any significant way is a mistake, especially if it has rust on the inside. The tank should be discarded and a replacement purchased. However, minor dents can sometimes be popped back from the inside with a homemade hammer. I have used a bronze golf putter with its shank bent to allow access to the dent through the gas tank opening. Use only a bronze putter to minimize spark danger inside the gas tank. This method works occasionally on larger tanks, but is difficult to apply to smaller tanks; and it only works with minor dents because it is tough to generate much force with this tool.

Starting tanks that have separated from the main tank should be reattached by a professional who knows how to braze and weld tanks that have held flammable liquids. DO NOT attempt any welding of the tank yourself—the risk of fire and explosion is very real!

FIT AND FINISH—LINING UP PANELS

Before you begin applying any coatings, attach the repaired panel to the tractor to evaluate its stance and flow of lines. It is very common for damaged panels that have been repaired to miss their mounting points by at least a little. Because it is the nature of metal to stretch when it is damaged and when it is worked and repaired, the fit and geometry of the piece has to be checked closely. We are not checking the finish of the piece or looking for surface imperfections; we are trying to evaluate its stance, its mounting, and the flow of its lines in relation to the tractor and other pieces. It should look right, tight, and straight, to paraphrase a bodyworker friend of mine. Especially look for interruptions in the flow of the lines of the sheet metal where two pieces meet.

After you have spent hours fixing and straightening, it is tough to find additional flaws when you make this inspection. But now is the time to find them, not after you have applied paint. If there ever was a certain point in the restoration where you should be a real stickler for details, this is it. Just remember to use steel's malleable characteristics to your advantage: stretch, heat, and hammer it out to make it thinner. If it needs to be shrunk, use shrinking-type body hammers and/or the heat and quench method. Remount the piece, evaluate its stance and flow of lines, and rework as necessary until you are sure all imperfections are removed.

After you have finished your repairs, are satisfied with the fit of the piece, and have cleaned the piece thoroughly enough to eat off it, you'll want to get the surface as smooth as possible. Use modern, lightweight, epoxy/fiber body fillers to fill all of the minor surface imperfections left behind by surface rust and bodywork.

Modern body fillers contain two separate components: a base and a catalyst. The base remains a gel until the catalyst is added, which causes the base to begin hardening. The hardening process occurs rapidly when a lot of catalyst is added. Add too much catalyst and the base hardens before you can even work with it; add too little catalyst and the process takes a long time. The trick is to follow the instructions carefully and mix a few test batches first to get the hang of your particular product.

Once you mix the two parts thoroughly, apply the body filler with a spatula in long strokes using firm, steady pressure. After the filler has dried enough to sand—usually about 30-60 minutes, depending on how well you mixed the filler components—begin sanding the body filler smooth. If the filler gums up your sandpaper, it's not ready to sand and needs to sit awhile longer. Filler should be sanded smooth with a long block sander equipped with 300-grit sandpaper. Use long, smooth strokes over the body filler, extending the strokes well past the body filler. After a short while, the edges of the filler will be "feathered" and will lap evenly and smoothly to metal. The area where metal stops and filler starts should be unnoticeable to the touch; use an air gun and tack cloth to remove the dust. Set up the piece in your painting area, and you're ready to apply the finish.

Remember, body filler is not a magic cure-all. In fact, most filler manufacturers explicitly limit their products' use to those circumstances where the filler will be no more than a few millimeters thick. It can be successfully applied thicker, especially in thin crevices with sharp, clean edges, but don't use body filler as a substitute for bodywork. If you have a depression in the metal, remove it with the manual methods outlined above before filling it. If you have a hole, fill it with a patch panel (or a spot weld if the hole is small). Body filler is for filling minor imperfections like grinding and sanding marks, imperfections from welds, and for those areas where additional bodywork will not yield any more benefit. If you find that you are applying it thickly and you can't get the metal any smoother with manual methods, you may want to consider buying a replacement piece instead. Body filler will fail over time, especially if the metal is flexed often, such as a fender that is always held on to when you climb aboard the tractor. For this reason, filler should be used sparingly.

A second glass of body fillers exist: glazing putties. This are very similar to body fillers but much thinner and lighter, and they are designed to be used after the painting process starts. You'll need glazing putty to fill imperfections that filler primers cannot correct (or require too many coats to correct) or to correct minor nicks and scratches accidentally created after painting starts. Glazing putty is very handy and I typically use it at least once to fill those rust pits I missed earlier or that grinding mark that was deeper than I expected.

Bodywork, like most work in restoration, is not outside the grasp of most people; it is almost as much an art as it is a craft. The rewards go to those who watch their material closely and work within each piece's set of behaviors and limitations. Try to develop new and creative ways to shape the metal and use the full range of your tools and skills. Don't be afraid to drop the obvious tool or technique and try something different if the obvious isn't working. It simply requires patience, creativity, and maybe a little help from a professional bodyshop when you run into a really difficult circumstance. Saving your sheet metal will create a sense of accomplishment, save you money, and make your tractor more original.

Tips & Tricks

• Find an artist's palette to use for mixing body filler or epoxy. It is easy to hold one-handed as you apply the material. Inexpensive palettes can be found at art supply stores.

• Body filler should be used to fill shallow rust damage, pinholes, and welding and grinding marks. It's not designed to be a replacement for bodywork; however, if you need more than a few millimeters of body filler to eliminate a flaw, then you should try to smooth the flaw further.

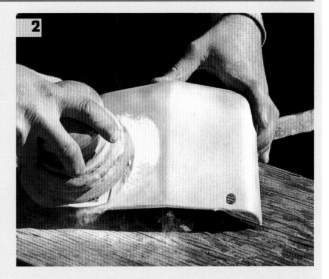

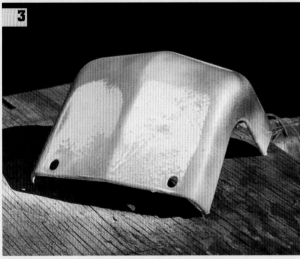

This is probably a nose section from a John Deere G. The section was very rusty and dented, and required a good bit of bodywork and sandblasting. Between the bodywork and rust pits, the surface required a coat of body filler. In picture 1, the body filler has already been applied, and a light coat of primer sprayed on top to act as a sanding guide. Next, Joey Kline works his sander over the areas where body filler was applied, keeping the pneumatic sander moving at all times (2). The first pass at sanding reveals the high and low spots. At the low spots, the primer dusting still exists; filler is exposed in the high spots (3). More sanding is needed to smooth out the surface (4). Joey continues sanding until he is satisfied that the surface is perfectly smooth, or until he is convinced he'll need to add a bit more body filler. In the last photograph (5), you can see how the right side smoothed out nicely, but the left side needs more sanding. The last step is to remove filler from mounting holes and seams and give the entire unit one last light sanding. Very small remaining blemishes can be corrected with a thinner filler called glazing putty. After this, a few more coats of filler primer will be applied, then a sealer coat, and the nosepiece is ready for paint.

Cosmetic Restoration

One of the fastest ways to start an argument at a John Deere antique tractor show is to proclaim the merits of one set of John Deere paint codes or one brand of paints over another. There are several reasons for this. The paint on an antique John Deere is the most visible part of the restoration; it is always a source of conversation and debate. It seems as if there should be a clear-cut answer, so anyone who has spent time researching it believes they know the answer. Regardless of what the "experts" say, clear answers to the "right" paint and color usage are elusive. The issue also is clouded by much misinformation.

The first misconception is that lacquer should be used because it predated enamel in carriage, automobile, and tractor painting. This is wrong; John Deere always used enamels on its tractors. Therefore, modern alkyd, acrylic, and acrylic-modified alkyd enamels are authentic to use in your tractor restoration.

The second misconception is that there is "one" correct shade of John Deere green and yellow. Although this is generally true, nothing could be further from the truth when you start talking about specific years and models. In the automotive industry, paint codes and formulas were better documented and more strictly followed in the production process. This strict adherence did not exist at John Deere or most other tractor manufacturers, nor do paint formulas exist in the company archives for every production year, vendor, or batch of paint. The shade slightly varied over the years as John Deere changed paint vendors, and the shade varied even between batches of paint from the same manufacturer.

If applying a flawlessly accurate shade of paint is important to you, then you should try to find areas of paint on your tractor that are large enough and in good enough condition for your paint supplier to match. Only then will you have the correct shade of paint for your tractor. To get a good color match, find a painted area that has not been exposed to the sun or heat, or darkened by exposure to oil, grease, or dirt. Often the bottoms of brackets or mounts, where the bottom is mated to another flat surface, are good places to look.

Clean and polish the area thoroughly and then take it to your paint supplier. A good paint supplier will use optical technology to arrive at a dead-on formulation based on your sample.

If painfully accurate paint is not your cup of tea and you would rather buy a premixed paint, then you probably want to know which exact color and make of paint to buy. First, there are two shades of John Deere green. There is a modern green, which the company introduced during the New Generation tractors in the 1960s, and there is a classic or antique green. When buying paint, just remember to ask for the classic formulation; paint suppliers will likely have both shades.

There are several brands of paint you can use. Of course there is the old stand-by, classic green and yellow from John Deere. This is John Deere's answer to the great color dilemma, and many folks claim it's the most accurate paint you can buy. For every advocate of John Deere paint, you'll find a detractor that claims the color is wrong—at least for specific model lines or years. Just about any purchased paint, unless you are lucky, will not exactly match your particular tractor.

You'll find other issues under debate at shows across the country, from whether you should use a simple enamel finish or a urethane base coat/clear coat system, to the source and application of decals, I suggest one response to these issues: It's your tractor. Your goals, tastes, and needs have to dictate the final answers. If you want a modern urethane base coat/clear coat system, that's what you should use. The advice and procedures in this chapter can be used for any finishing system. Just be sure you understand your objectives and safety concerns, and make decisions. To help make your decisions, you can search for answers at tractor shows or on the Internet. Seek out the tractors, owners, and restorers whose work you admire and trust and ask them what products and paints they used. Based on their responses and your objectives, you'll arrive at answers that will help you create a restoration you will admire for a lifetime.

Tips & Tricks
• A paint shaker is a great machine to have if you can find a used one cheaply enough. It's not handy enough to spend lots of money on, though.

Setting Up the Paint Gun

Applying paint well requires that the paint gun is provided with the proper air pressure and volume. The spray gun product literature is the best source for this information. The documentation that comes with your paint may indicate it too, but your gun manufacturer best knows the proper psi for its product. Lacking this documentation, I recommend 40-50 psi for regular spray guns. HVLP conversion guns require similar pressures, but some require as high as 70 psi, and they require considerable air volume. Test your gun with air to be sure your compressor can keep up. If your compressor constantly runs but pressure steadily drops, your compressor is not large enough. You will be able to spray only for short periods of time before you have to stop and let the air compressor catch up.

When setting the pressure in your air supply for your paint gun, put a pressure gauge on the gun, and hook the air supply and any filter you plan on using with the gun to the gauge. The gauge at the gun should read 40-50 psi; it's irrelevant what the gauge reads at the tank regulator. The hose, the inline filter, and other factors will decrease pressure at the gun. For example, at my shop, depending on the hose and filters I use and how dirty the filter is, I must set the tank side regulator for 52 to 65 psi to get 45 psi at the gun. Setting your pressure this way will assure you of proper pressures.

Tips & Tricks

• Remember to devise methods to hang up parts for painting before you start painting. I use coat hangers for light parts and picture wire or mechanic's wire for heavier parts. A clothes rack bought from a yard sale makes a great frame to hang parts.

• Use steel or wooden rods to support heavy cast items when painting them. For example, axle housings can be completely painted if you use a steel rod placed through the housing and supported by jacks at both ends.

My Painting System

What do I use? When it come to finishes, my approach can be summed up like this: I am not a paint snob; I am a pragmatic painter that tends toward authenticity, so take my advice or don't. I don't use the latest, cutting-edge urethane paints—mainly for safety reasons, though there are aesthetic reasons as well—nor do I use clear coats. Having said that, I also am not a purist, someone who might say that using primer on a tractor is not truly original (John Deere didn't prime until very late into the Two-Cylinder years). I want my paint to protect the tractor for a very long time so I can use any coating or additive that will enhance the lifetime of the finish without detracting from creating a build, color, and gloss that looks and feels original, as much as possible. I prefer PPG's line of Light Industrial undercoatings combined with John Deere's classic shades of paint. The classic formulations from John Deere are close to original and very consistent (the batch I picked up this year was identical to the batch I picked up two years ago), and its use is easy to defend to the armchair restorers at the tractor shows. I have matched PPG paint to my specific shade before, too, and I really liked the results even though the extra trouble didn't seem worth it. John Deere used to sell only alkyd enamel, which is soft and very slow to dry. Now it sells paint in acrylic form and the paint dries much more quickly and is tougher.

On sheet metal and pieces of cast steel, I first etch with phosphoric acid wash, then use an epoxy primer. On cast iron, I prime with the nonepoxy primer recommended for the painting system that I am using (usually a vinyl-acrylic primer). I always apply two or three coats of this primer. On sheet metal—but typically on very little else—use primer-surfacer to help build the coating, sanding between coats with a long block sander. I repeat this until I have a finish that is as smooth and blemish-free as possible. Then I apply a sealer on top of this. On top of the sealer I apply the color coats, building up the finish with two or three coats. If the color coats aren't as smooth or as built-up as I would like, I'll shoot another two or three coats in the next painting session. I add hardeners, and if gloss is too high, I add flattening pastes, but I haven't needed it in the greens (but have in the colors of other makes of tractors). That's it—no urethanes, clear coats, or anything obnoxiously dangerous; just these simple three coatings and a few additives.

Tips & Tricks

• Material Safety Data Sheets (MSDS) sheets are available for every finishing product you buy. The vendor is required to make them available at every point of sale. If they don't, be sure to ask for them. They contain valuable safety and first-aid information.

PAINTING PRODUCTS

They are many different categories of finishing products, and all are required to create a long-lasting finish that goes on smooth and trouble-free. To understand these products, it helps to keep in mind that a complete finishing system is really nothing more than a set of products that work together to create a very hard skin that adheres to your tractor like glue. After painting many layers, the layers of the different products meld into a monolithic coat. To accomplish this, you must use coatings that chemically react to each other and fuse together, essentially becoming one layer. Only the primer coat actually sticks to the tractor's underlying surface (the metal); all of the other coats chemically bond to the previous coat. The filler coat "melts" into the primer and becomes part of the primer after curing; the color coats melt into the filler coats, and so on. That is why following instructions about drying times, recoat times, and the use of compatible products are so important. Otherwise, all you'll have are a bunch of coats that "stick" to each other like multiple layers of wallpaper, at best. At worst, you'll have created a real mess. Compatible, melded-together coats create a much stronger and better-looking finish.

PAINTING PRODUCTS

Here is John Deere's primer/sealer. This primer has very little filling and building characteristics, and is designed to be the first coating on the metal to protect it and form a foundation for other coats. Most folks will follow this primer with a compatible building primer to build up the finish and smooth out very minor surface blemishes.

The following is a sample of three commonly used brands of paint. The top is John Deere's classic green; bottom left is Martin Senour's (sold through NAPA), and Dupont's Centari. All offer a great-looking John Deere green and yellow, and all perform well. The John Deere paint is your best bet for color consistency and accuracy, although the other two are better paints and more easily obtained. Ultimately, the choice is yours.

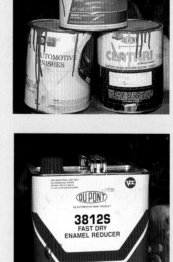

Paint additives you may consider include a hardener. While all hardeners enhance the gloss of the paint to a degree, the one on the left includes gloss-enhancing agents that add more gloss. While there is no packaging standard in this regard, most of these types of hardeners will include some type of labeling (i.e., "Wet Look") to indicate that gloss levels will be higher than you might normally expect from a hardener. Ask for a freshly sprayed sample, or experiment with different brands until you find a hardener that performs the way you want it to.

Reducers are additives that alter the way paint flashes off and dries. Paint cures and dries differently depending on temperature and humidity, and a reducer must be added to compensate. For example, this reducer is a fast-dry reducer, meaning you would use it on chilly, damp days to speed up the flash and dry times. On hot, dry days you would use a slow-dry reducer. Your paint supplier can give you better recommendations regarding proportions and the type of reducer for your circumstance.

ETCHING COATS: Etching coats are nothing more than acids applied to bare metals. This is entirely optional; some primers are self-etching, so using an etching coat is redundant. Etching coats improve the adhesion of the primer and provide a small measure of protection against flash rust that might begin to occur on the bare metal between cleaning and applying primer. These etching products are typically phosphoric or muriatic acid-based coatings that are sprayed, brushed, or rubbed on with a sponge. A brand of gelled phosphoric acid called Naval Jelly is excellent for its low water content and ease of cloth wiping. I prefer an etching coat provided by the primer manufacturer. It's only slightly more expensive than buying the acids outright, and ensures compatibility between the etching and primer.

ADHESION PRIMERS: Adhesion primers are designed to act like glue, thinned to a paintable consistency, and formulated to be chemically compatible with the fillers and color coats that follow. They are formulated for very high adhesion, at the expense of looks or build of the finish. The many types of primers have their strong points and drawbacks; which one you use is best recommended by the vendors of your finishing system. Epoxy is the best all-around performer for initial primer coats, especially on sheet metal. After applying a few coats, it is nonporous and completely protects the metal. Its primary drawback is its high cost. Vinyl acrylic and other related enamel primers and lacquer primers adhere well, but not as well as epoxy primer. On rough surfaces such as cast iron, where adhesion by all primers is generally excellent, epoxy may be overkill and less-expensive primers can be used. Epoxy has a shorter topcoat window, usually about seven days. That means you have less than a week to start applying filler primers or color coat. If you wait longer, you have to mechanically abrade the primer and reapply it before you continue. The other primers typically are more lenient and give you more time. None of these adhesion-type primers fill very well; that is, all surface imperfections will telescope through the primer and be quite noticeable.

FILLER PRIMERS: Filler primers are designed to create a filling effect and build up the finish. When sanded between coats, they build up a finish that is smooth and blemish-free. On sheet metal, where an exceptionally smooth surface is needed, this primer is very important to fill the minor blemishes caused by rust and left behind by bodywork. On cast iron, which is supposed to retain its rough texture after painting, it isn't really necessary, though some folks put on a coat or two to minimize the rough appearance or to correct heavy rust damage. Other pieces, such as stamped- and cast-steel pieces, typically aren't coated with filler primers either, but you'll need to take each piece on a case-by-case basis.

When applying filler primers on sheet metal, you should sand between each coat with a long block-style sander. Continued application of the filler, followed by sanding after each coat, will create a flawlessly smooth finish. Many restorers apply two different colors of filler primer, alternating colors with each coat. Then, as you sand between each coat, the color of the previous coat will be exposed at the high places and the color of the most recent coat will remain in the low places. This accentuates and exposes the high and low areas on the metal and alerts you to problem areas in the finish. After you have built the primer-surfacer to the point where the surface is smooth and even (usually requiring two to eight coats, depending on thickness of each coat, condition of the metal, etc.), you can fill any remaining flaws with glazing putty. Sand the glazing putty with your block sander, then paint a light dusting of primer-surfacer. Give everything one final light sanding and clean the metal thoroughly with a tack cloth. The sanding process may have left some small areas of metal exposed along ridges, edges, or other areas with a positive relief. This is OK, as long as you apply sealer as soon as you are finished.

SEALERS: Sealers are special coatings designed to seal the primer and any metal that might be exposed. This step is particularly important if you use filler primers because their porosity will telescope through the color coat, giving it a granular or speckled appearance. Very light sanding of the sealer is not recommended unless application of the sealer was incorrect and re-application is necessary.

PAINTS: Enamels and urethanes are the two primary paints you need to consider. Enamel paints are the least expensive, most original, and, in their modern formulations, produce finishes that rival urethanes. There are three primary types of enamel: alkyd, acrylic, and a hybrid of the two. Alkyd enamels are the enamel paints of yesteryear and are the most authentic for your tractor. They are slow to dry and are soft, but they build up quickly and give a very nice, glossy finish. These paints still have their place, and originality demands this type of paint. Acrylic enamels are harder, stand up better to weather, UV rays, and abuse, and build glossier finishes, but are more expensive. The hybrid—acrylic-modified alkyd enamel—is a mixture the two and its advantages and drawbacks are compromises of the two. I have used acrylic modified alkyd enamel quite a bit on other tractors and cars and like them. It seems to have the build and cost characteristics of alkyd enamels while exhibiting much of the same durability and gloss of acrylic enamel. Usually which type of enamel you use is constrained by the manufacturer of the paint, so you may not have a choice. For example, John Deere's paint is acrylic enamel and no other types of enamel exist. All enamels benefit from the addition of a hardener because it will mitigate the only drawback of enamel, —it is not as hard as other paint types, such as urethane. I recommend an acrylic or acrylic-modified enamel for your restoration.

Urethanes are better paints—there's no doubt about it. They are more dangerous to apply than unhardened enamels, however, and more costly to purchase. I don't recommend their use, especially to first-time restorers. Making mistakes and spilling paint is troublesome enough, but it is especially vexing when each mistake or spill consumes a noticeable amount of money. If you want to use clear coat on your tractor, a urethane base coat/clear coat system is the most foolproof choice for an amateur. Clear coat can be used on enamel, but I find enamels tough to apply as you start blending in the clear coat. Again, a really patient full-service paint supply store is your best friend when making these choices.

ADDITIVES: There are several additives available to consider before you start painting. The first, and the one I recommend using, is hardener. This additive gives the paint an extra durability and should be added to all color coats. Hardeners contain isocyanates, which add a certain measure of personal risk (see sidebar). The risk is not as significant as when using urethane paints, but isocyanates do require high-quality respirators and adequate ventilation. Hardeners increase the gloss of the paint noticeably, giving it a deep gloss. This gloss level may be unacceptable if a truly authentic restoration is done. If so, the next additive can be used.

FLATTENING PASTE: Flattening paste is an additive primarily composed of gypsum or talc. Its role is to reduce the gloss level of the paint (the paint used on old tractors is not as glossy as modern paints). It is optional and not widely used. Flattening paste is best added during the paint-matching phase at the paint supplier, but if you bought the paint premixed, you can add it by trial and error. You can mix up several small batches of paint and apply these mixtures to test panels (poster board works well for this purpose) to determine what gloss level suits your needs best.

CLEAR COAT: If a super high gloss with a "wet" look is what you're after, using this additive is the way to go. Clear coat is used by adding it in small amounts to the last few color coats, then topping this with a coat or two of reduced clear coat. After this, you "mist" the finish with a highly thinned coat of clear coat additive. This can be done on either enamel or urethane.

THINNERS AND REDUCERS: Thinners are used primarily for cleaning, and are not used during painting with automotive-grade paints. They are handy for removing unwanted paint and removing sags and runs from the paint while it's still wet. Reducers are almost chemically identical to thinners. In fact, thinners can be used as reducers, but this isn't recommended. Reducers are formulated to be identical to the solvent base used in the paint and work using smaller amounts, which prevents the ratio of solvent to solids in the paint from increasing as much as it might with a thinner.

Reducers are necessary because the application characteristics of paint change with humidity and temperature. In cool and humid conditions, paint "flashes off" (becomes tacky and no longer flows) slowly, and it is hard to prevent sags and runs. In hot, low-humidity situations, paint flashes off almost immediately, leading to a gritty, lackluster finish. Reducers change the rate at which paint flashes off, allowing you to compensate for temperature and humidity. This improves the application characteristics of the paint and makes it easier to apply the paint in all circumstances. Many weekend restorers assume they don't need to worry about reducers, but anything that improves the application characteristics of the paint makes us better painters. It also allows us to paint in circumstances when we might not ordinarily get to paint, such as in the cool of the evening after work, or on hot Saturday afternoons.

Tips & Tricks

• Adding hardener to paint substantially increases its gloss level. Talk with your paint supplier about the likelihood of a recommended hardener adding too much gloss to the finished product. They may recommend flattening the paint slightly with flattening paste to reach an acceptable gloss level.

Common Painting Flaws

The following is a list of common painting problems (other than drips, runs, and sags) and their likely causes. Virtually all of them can be traced to one of four things: Contaminants in the new paint, or on the surface you are painting; paint that is improperly reduced or thinned; paint that is applied too thickly; or not following recoat times. Common sources of contaminants are from wax on old paint, or water or oil in the air supply. Most flaws require that the paint be tacked off before they are noticeable, but some are noticeable right away. Repair of these flaws always means allowing the paint to cure enough to sand, sanding off the affected area, and trying again. If you see the problem while the paint is wet and the area affected is small, you may be able to remove the flaw by wiping the area with a rag soaked in solvent, shooting the area with paint again. This method works only when the coat you are shooting is not the final coat. If the paint has tacked off before you noticed the problem, then wait approximately 24 to 36 hours, sand the affected area, and reapply paint to the entire piece.

Fisheye: This looks like small craters with soft, rounded rims in your paint. The most common cause for this condition is a surface that was not adequately cleaned. In particular, this can be caused by residue of waxes on the old paint.

Orange peel: When the paint seems littered with very small dimples (you may mistake it for a slightly rough surface) that looks a little like the skin of an orange, you have a condition called orange peel. Amateurs usually see this in their work when they apply the coat of paint too thin. More experienced painters create this by not reducing the paint enough for the temperature present during paint application.

Chipping: If the paint chips easily, one or more layers of the coating system failed. This is usually seen in small clusters and is caused by the metal not being cleaned properly. The areas that were not cleaned (missed or inadequately cleaned) will leave bare metal exposed when they chip. If the chips expose other coatings (primer or paint), the cause is usually an undercoat that was allowed to cure too long before additional coats were applied.

No gloss or luster: This is almost always caused by inadequate reducing or paint applied too thinly. It can also be caused by a primer coating that was not sealed when it should have been. Certain additives, like hardener, that are contaminated (mainly from moisture drawn from the air) will cause this too.

Wrinkling: This is caused when additional coats are applied after the previous layer has had time to tack off but not to cure solidly. Recoating should happen after the paint has flashed (the paint's surface solvents have evaporated), but the surface is still tacky. If you miss this recoat window of opportunity, wait 24 to 36 hours before trying to recoat.

Nearly all of the problems listed above may also be caused by improper mixing of components or coating systems. Once again, be sure to read and follow, to the letter, the application guidelines for the coatings you are using.

CLEANUP

Cleanup is usually done with lacquer thinner or xylol, but consult the product label of the finish you are using to find the recommended cleaner. All cleaners require a respirator and gloves during use.

Start by cleaning the spray gun first. Take two buckets, the cleaner, an empty, sealable container, the tools, and the spray gun (still attached to an air supply) outside. Fill the paint tank on the gun half full with cleaner, reattach the tank, and then slosh it around several times. Detach the tank and pour the contents into one bucket. Do this a few times until the tank is clean. Fill the tank again, reattach it, and spray cleaner through the gun into the second bucket until nothing but clear cleaner comes out.

Disassemble the paint gun and wipe all of the parts with clean cleaner. Add some more cleaner to the first bucket and fill the second bucket with enough cleaner to submerge all paint-covered tools. Take each tool and do a rough first cleaning in the first bucket, followed by a final soak and cleaning in the second bucket. After everything is squeaky clean, let the pieces air-dry outside and then pour the contents of the buckets into the empty sealable container. If allowed to sit for a day or two, the paint will settle at the bottom of the cleaner container, allowing you to carefully pour clear cleaner back into its original container. This system of cleaning will maximize the use of cleaner, minimize how often you need to dispose of dirty cleaner, and save money in the process.

SUPPLIES

The list of available gadgets for finishing work is long, but most are optional and some are even downright

Xylol and lacquer thinner pull double duty. They can both be used as a reducer, in a pinch (they don't perform as well as reducers designed for your paint), but more typically are used for clean up.

ridiculous. In addition to the consumable supplies you'll need during sanding and repair, there are many other helpful items. You'll want to have tack cloths (prepackaged cloths infused with a tacky substance for removing sanding and other dust), a lot of clear plastic mixing cups with volume gradations (usually free from the paint supplier), drip-proof spouts for your paint cans, and lots of rubber gloves. To mask off areas that are not to be painted, be sure to have masking tape and masking paper (newspaper works well). Be sure you ask for those free mixing sticks from your paint supplier.

PUTTING IT ALL TOGETHER

Regardless of the paint you choose, using a system of paints means that all of your coatings—the primer, primer-surfacer, color coat, and additives—are compatible with, and designed for, each other. These systems should be bought from one product line and from one vendor. If that is impossible (for instance, you want to use John Deere's paint but another make of primer), be sure to buy the color coat first and have it on hand so

you can show it to the supplier of the undercoatings. The supplier can then recommend undercoatings that are compatible with your paint or, at the very least, what coatings you'll have to use between the undercoatings and color coat to make them compatible. Be sure to obtain a set of application guidelines and material safety data sheets for all products. These documents contain indispensable application and safety information.

Cosmetic Restoration

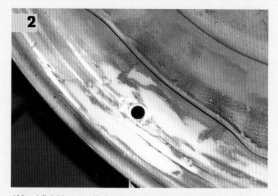

Tractor painting involves very little finesse in terms of masking and edge painting. There are a few areas that will have to be masked off; especially if your tractor is a 30-series with a two-tone paint job. Masking tape and paper are used often; very fine, thin masking tape is necessary from time to time to get that crisp, sharp border between paint colors.

Wheel finishing usually involves a lot of sandblasting and body filler. Wheels are typically heavily rusted, and often, liquid ballast has seeped out and begun to rust out the part of the rim near the valve stem. Here, you can see that body filler was required around the stem because of leaking calcium-chloride ballast. It doesn't show well in the photograph, but a square section around the stem was removed and a new piece welded in. Some of the body filler is filling the minor blemishes that grinding and welding leaves behind.

This is the only sane way to paint wheels with tires mounted. These steel bands, and a little bit of care, will keep the paint off of the tires, yet still get paint on the outside edge of the rim.

Painting wheels—especially spoke wheels—can be tough, and wastes paint. There are two strategies that help. First, set up your spray gun to shoot a tall, narrow, vertical pattern; this is especially helpful with spoke wheels. Second, follow the old adage about cleaning a room: "Clean the corners of the room and the center will take care of itself." Joey Kline, of Kline Restorations, is following this advice by painting the disc/rim junction area first. This approach will help prevent the accumulation of too much paint in one area, which can create runs and sags or missing areas.

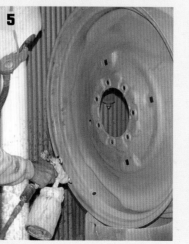

When painting a wheel, prime the tire portion of the rim, but don't paint it. Here Joey is applying epoxy primer to the wheel. When you apply the primer, apply it to the tire part of the rim first.

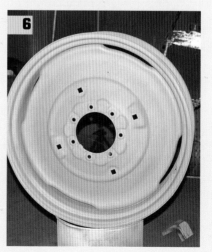

Here is the wheel, complete with its first coat of epoxy primer. This primer is best applied in one full, complete, wet coat; a second if needed after the first has flashed off. Do not try to build up epoxy primer with multiple coats.

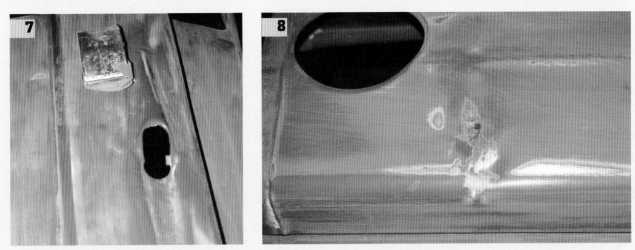

What do you do if you want to apply a new coat of paint to your tractor but the existing paint is not terribly old and adhering well to the metal? As long as the current coat is not too thick, your best bet is to simply sand it very well, clean it very thoroughly, and then fix the blemishes as shown in photograph (7). Apply a sealer next, then apply building primer (as thin as possible in this case), a sealer, and then your finish coat. There is no need to strip the existing paint if it is a fairly recent and solid coat of paint. The operative words are sanding and cleaning—make sure you do both well.

Mixing modern paints will leave you feeling like a chemist in a laboratory. To mix most enamel paint, first read the application guide that comes with the paint and additives. They will state the proportions to be used when adding reducer and hardener. Next, using a graduated cup marked with proportions, start by adding paint to the cup (9) Add your reducer next (10). Notice that the painter in the photograph is using a warm-weather reducer; he painted on a hot, humid August day. This reducer will prolong the time it takes the paint to flash off, preventing a lackluster, gritty finish associated with paint that flashed off too quickly. After adding the hardener (11), and stirring well (12) pour the paint into the gun cup, straining it with a paper strainer (a freebie from your paint supplier) to remove any large particles that got into the paint (13).

Cosmetic Restoration

Epoxy primer is a 50/50 mix between a base and a catalyst. Shown in 14 is a handy graduated mixing stick. You can use the marks on the stick to measure the pour (15); then use it to stir the paint. This tool gives you another benefit: no additional mixing cups to clean. When mixing epoxy, pour the base first, then add the catalyst (16).

There are two difficult aspects of painting a tractor: Every exposed surface is painted, and you cannot paint many exposed surfaces while they are mounted to the tractor. In the following collection of shots are some tips and tricks that will help you get the job done, with a minimum of fuss. To start, this photograph from Kline Restorations shows a couple important points. First, fasteners can be hand painted, if needed, after items are installed. Next, not every little thing was, or should be, painted. The brake-adjusting nut here is not painted and will remain unpainted.

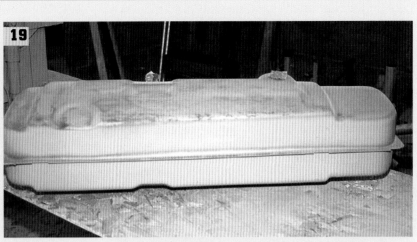

Large collections of small parts are much easier to paint if you set them up on a mesh surface. The mesh prevents a build-up of paint under the parts and keeps spray bounce-back to a minimum.

Originally, gas tanks on styled tractors were not painted well at the factory (often the bottom got paint but the top didn't). Most restorers will paint the tanks as if they will be visible. Here, this tank receives its primer coat. Gas tanks should be painted in two stages; first one side, then the other. It's tempting to mount a gas tank using the filler hole on a short pole and paint it all at once. I suspect that the weight of some tanks may be enough to dent or bend the metal around the filler hole, so I don't recommend it.

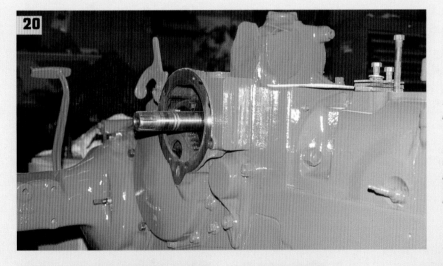

How far should the tractor be disassembled or assembled before painting begins? The next three pictures give you an idea of what some of the professional restorers do. In photograph 20, some of the mechanical systems are there, like the governor housing, but the axle housings were painted off of the tractor to allow brake assembly after paint. Photograph 21 shows how far a John Deere H was taken down before it was sandblasted and primed. In photograph 22, note the wood template used to mask and seal the cylinder block opening in the main case of a Model H. Tape and/or paper spanning such a large area would surely tear or fail after a short while.

PREP AND PAINT (CONTINUED)

This next set of shots shows handy ways to paint tractor parts. These methods are well-suited for bulky or long parts. In 23 it looks like washday with all the parts lined up to dry. Next, you can see the best way to paint a flywheel (24). The flywheel is placed on a pole that is held up in an engine stand. Flywheels are so heavy that this arrangement is about the only one that works. Likewise for the radiator (25), holding it with stout chains is the only safe way to hang it. The chain attachment points will be touched up when the radiator is mounted to the tractor. Many parts have areas that get paint and areas that don't; here (26), a portion of the lift arm gets masked before painting. The next photograph shows why you should disassemble as far you can before painting (27). The starter rod spring and bushing was left on, leaving painting shadows that will have to be touched up.

In photograph 28, the battery box bottom was painted (trailing edges of the paint-spray pattern can be seen at the bottom) before it was mounted. This was done because parts of the bottom are visible and painting them with the box mounted is difficult to do well. Painting tractor sheet metal is what folks think about when they think of finishing the restoration. This is the final sprint to the finish line, but don't rush. This work is the most visible, and the part you have to look at for years to come. I chose a 520 hood, grille and nosepiece as the subjects for these photographs because they have everything you may run across: Two-tone paint, difficult-to-reach areas, lots of surface area and two-sided painting. The first two pictures (29 and 30) show the work of Rich "Bud" Johannsen of Lost Art Body and Paint as he has finished the bodywork, priming and the yellow portions of the sheet metal, using masking techniques. Bud is masking the yellow portions of the hood in photo 31; very narrow tape must be used to define the border. Wide tape leaves lines that are only as straight as the edge of the tape, whereas, narrow tape is as straight as you make it. They are backed up by wider tape and the surface is blown off.

continued on next page

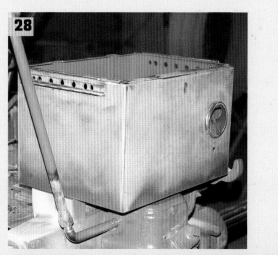

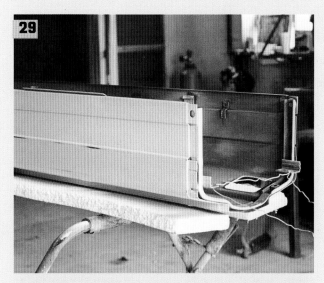

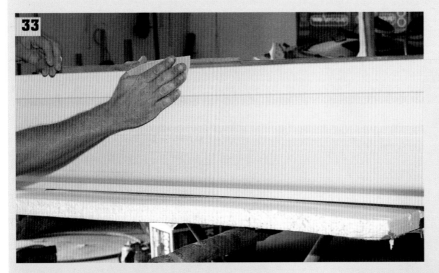

Final, light sanding commences (33). Why sand after taping? The tape will help protect the yellow from an errant swipe from the sandpaper.
Bud takes pains to sand every square inch in the next three photographs (34-36), being sure to sand all the way up to the tape. Some metal showing through will be normal at the raised areas after sanding. Because the last step before the color coat is to seal the primer, the metal will be sealed also and none of this will affect paint adhesion. After sanding, the rest of the yellow is masked in 37; you can do this earlier when the other masking is done.

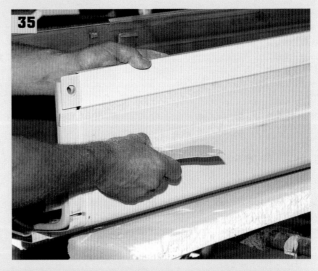

Next, Bud has hung the hood (38) in the spraying area so he can reach all areas in one pass. He used holes that are hidden when the hood is installed to hang the hood. Before sealing, the surface is thoroughly cleaned with a cleaner that is designed to remove all traces of contaminants that threaten paint quality and adhesion. To prevent dust from kicking up during painting, the floor and lower walls are wet down (39). The sealer coat is then applied (40). Use a sealer color different enough from your primers so you can easily see that all areas are covered. After the sealer has had time to flash off (not long for most sealers) the color coat is applied. Here (41) Bud puts on two wet coats. He'll follow up with additional coats, as needed, to build color and gloss (42).

PREP AND PAINT (CONTINUED)

Next, we'll do the grille and nose of the tractor. This photograph (43) shows how rounded corners are masked. Trim the tape, as necessary, to finish out the rounding effect. Sanding was done before Bud finished off the masking, using paper on the larger areas. Once again, thoroughly clean the sheet metal before spraying the sealer in 44-46. Then spray the color coat (47). Photograph 48 shows an even, glossy, blemish-free finish. This is the result of care, patience, and an unwillingness to accept anything less than a flawless finish. It may take some practice, and you may have to sand and repaint a mistake or two, but creating a great finish is possible if you abide by these three rules.

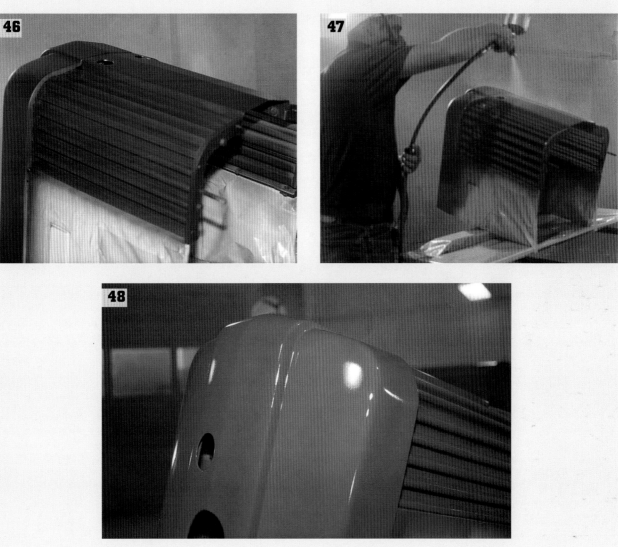

Tips & Tricks

• If your air compressor sends water and oil vapor to the spray gun, even if you have a filter at the compressor and a small filter at the gun, you may need to get an air drying system. This is a device designed to remove all water from an air stream. Smaller desiccant-based systems are more affordable but typically cannot deliver high air volumes. The more expensive systems are refrigerant-based systems that cool the air stream and will deliver high volumes of air.

Safety

There are several nonintuitive dangers present when using modern painting products. First, they are highly flammable. Spraying paint is like spraying a fine mist of gasoline in the air. Any open source of ignition will ignite the vapors, causing a deadly fire and explosion. I know one person this happened to. He had a low fire burning in a wood stove way at the other end of the shop when he started applying paint. Halfway through the job, the vapors ignited, destroying half the shop and leaving the painter with second- and third-degree burns. Be sure you turn off all pilot lights and other open sources of ignition before painting.

Some types of paints and additives contain isocyanates, a type of cyanide. Urethane finishes that many people recommend for use on antique tractors contain high levels of isocyanates. The hardeners that you add to enamel paint also contain isocyanates. Isocyanates are poisonous, and because everyone's level of sensitivity to cyanide is different, there is no easy way to determine how quickly you may react when exposed to isocyanates. Some people can apply paints with isocyanates while using normal respirators and never react to the small amounts that may make it through the respirator. Others react violently after very small exposures. Ideally, you should use what is called a fresh-air respirator if you use any paint that contains isocyanates. Fresh-air respirators provide fresh air to the respirator mask from an area that doesn't contain paint fumes. When properly used, they completely eliminate any risk of cyanide poisoning.

Handling: All paints, thinners, reducers, and cleaners require splash-proof goggles, appropriate rubber gloves, and long-sleeved shirts when handling and mixing. Most of these products are absorbed through the skin—especially the light solvents like thinners and reducers. They cause central nervous system, liver, and kidney damage, and some of the damage is accumulative. Your health and safety are not worth any antique tractor. To minimize spillage, use the drip-proof spouts that you can buy to install on your paint cans. Immediately clean up spills with rags and hang them outside to dry; do not pile them in a corner—this is a fire hazard. Do not store chemicals in areas accessible to children or in areas where they will be exposed to freezing temperatures. When these types of chemicals need to be discarded, dispose of them at your town or county's hazardous waste facility; never pour them on the ground.

Respiration: All modern painting products require respirators during handling and application. The dust mask you might use when mowing grass or when installing insulation is not an acceptable respirator. Proper respirators look a little like the gas masks World War I soldiers wore. They cover your mouth and nose and have screw-in filters that should be replaced periodically. These can be purchased from the same place where you buy your finishing products.

One simple mantra will guide you in using your respirator and safety gear: Put them on before you open the first can of paint or solvent and don't take them off until after you have cleaned everything, the last can is closed, and the room has been properly ventilated. Make no exceptions, and always read and adhere to the precautions on the product labels.

Remember, applying paints is serious business. Never paint without a respirator or without reading the material safety data sheets that come with your painting products. Always use, store, and handle painting products as highly flammable materials.

Tips & Tricks

• Before painting in your shop, you can coat items vulnerable to overspray with an aerosol-type cooking oil (like Pam®). This is especially handy for windows, because you usually need the light and don't want to cover them with a tarp. The paint won't stick and the oil is easy to clean up afterward.

Respirator

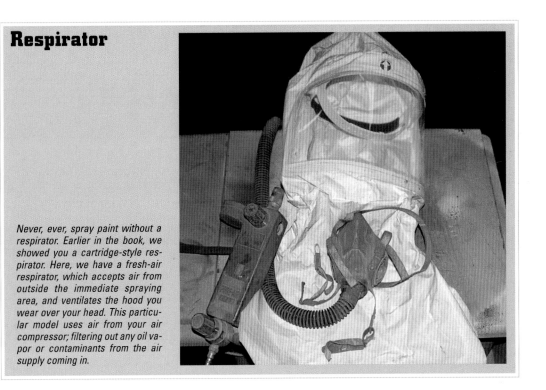

Never, ever, spray paint without a respirator. Earlier in the book, we showed you a cartridge-style respirator. Here, we have a fresh-air respirator, which accepts air from outside the immediate spraying area, and ventilates the hood you wear over your head. This particular model uses air from your air compressor; filtering out any oil vapor or contaminants from the air supply coming in.

DECALS

Applying decals to John Deere tractors is relatively easy. Hundreds of people have spent countless hours researching the correct size and placement of decals on every model of John Deere Two-Cylinder tractor. This work has borne fruit through the services and products of many decal providers whose decals are well made and accurate to the originals. If painfully accurate lettering and graphics are important to you, there are shops that will silk-screen the graphics to your sheet metal.

The suppliers of decals and silk-screen services can be found in the appendices, but one supplier deserves special mention. For years, Jorde Decals has unquestionably set the standard of originality for Mylar and vinyl decals. Jorde's patient and well-researched advice will answer your questions about placement, and they know which decals apply to your particular model. For example, diesel fuel tractors had some decals that the gas tractors didn't. Until recently, Jorde decals were the only decals worth buying, but within the last three or four years, a few other companies have emerged that offer decals whose accuracy and quality rivals those from Jorde.

Vinyl decals from most vendors feature individually cut lettering and accurate color, and their sets are 100 percent complete for most models. For general use, I recommend individually cut, letter vinyl decals sold on prespaced backing paper. These types of decals are the easiest to apply flawlessly, and vinyl lasts longer than any other type. If originality is important, Mylar decals are your best bet. If your tractor is older than 1941, and painfully accurate originality is important, then you should have some of your decals silk-screened.

MOVING AHEAD

I am convinced that almost everyone who hires out any part of his or her restoration hires out the wrong part. Most subcontract the painting, not realizing that creating a great finish is within almost everyone's grasp, and that painting is probably the most rewarding part of the restoration. Everything that you've done, and all of the work you've put in prior to painting, is strangely invisible. You can see it, but it doesn't look finished. Adding paint to your project brings it to life, makes it worthwhile, and signals its completion. Anyone willing to invest in good paint, paints patiently, and sands off mistakes and starts again can create a finish of beauty. In painting, there is no such thing as a permanent or too-expensive mistake. As long as the world makes sandpaper, you can erase your mistake and try again. With this chapter and a little persistence, you can be well on your way to a perfect finish.

Appendices

"Indeed, the best books have a use, like sticks and stones, which is above or beside their design, not anticipated in the preface, not concluded in the appendix."
—Henry David Thoreau

SOURCES OF JOHN DEERE INFORMATION

The most powerful way to find parts, fellow collectors, and manuals quickly is to use the Internet. I used to include links to Web sites with reference or historical data in the appendices of my books, but the proliferation of Web sites, the fluid nature of addresses, and the relatively short shelf life of many sites makes this no longer feasible. Go to my Web site (http://www.atis.net) and subscribe to the John Deere mailing list. There you will find fellow collectors who will discuss John Deere tractors with you. These collectors can best point you to the other Web sites that will meet your needs if mine doesn't.

INTERNET INFORMATION AND SERVICES

Antique Tractor Internet Services, 3160 MacBrandon Lane, Pfafftown, NC 27040; (336) 766-5255; http://www.atis.net. This Web site is owned by the author and was the first, and still is, the largest and most complete site on the Internet for all antique tractors. A specific area of the site is dedicated to John Deere enthusiasts. It specializes in providing World Wide Web services for antique tractor businesses, collectors, and clubs.

Don't overlook John Deere & Company. The John Deere Collectors Center, an institute of the John Deere Foundation, houses several exhibits, a museum, and the company archives. The archives are a fountain of knowledge for the restoration community. This information is not free, but the cost is reasonable and some free searches are available to subscribers of the official magazine of the collectors' center, *John Deere Traditions*. Visit http://www.JohnDeereCollectorsCtr.com for more information.

PERIODICALS

The following is a list of periodicals that deal specifically with the history of John Deere, or are a technical reference that covers—at least in part—John Deere Two-Cylinder tractors. All of the magazines with a circulation of greater than a few thousand are included here. *Antique Power, Green Magazine,* and *Two-Cylinder Magazine* have the largest circulation and largest number of advertisers and classified ads.

Antique Power, PO Box 562, Yellow Springs, OH 45387; (800) 767 5828; Pat Ertl (Publisher/Editor); free classifieds to subscribers.
All brands tractor magazine.

The Belt Pulley, PO Box 83, Nokomis, IL 62075. All brands tractor magazine.

Gas Engine Magazine, PO Box 328, Lancaster, PA 17608. For enthusiasts and collectors of all types of gasoline engines.

Green Magazine, Route 1, PO Box 7, Bee, NE 68314. For John Deere enthusiasts.

Polk's, 72435 SR 15, New Paris, IN 46553. All brands tractor magazine.

Two-Cylinder Club, 310 East G Avenue, Grundy Center, IA 50638. Annual membership includes the magazine.

ESSENTIAL JOHN DEERE BOOKS

Not all titles of John Deere books are included here. This is a short list of essential books every John Deere restorer and collector should have in his or her library. In addition to the books listed, you should purchase any history or reference books that deal specifically with the model of tractor you own. *John Deere Tractors and Equipment, Volumes I and II.* I wholeheartedly recommend these books. If I could have only one John Deere book, one of these would suffice.

John Deere Data Book. Quick reference on the details of tractor models.
Original John Deere Letter Series Tractors 1923-1954. A restoration and identification guide that is more in-depth than the other books.

Illustrated John Deere Two-Cylinder Tractor Buyer's Guide. Good book for the first-timer to use when comparing tractors at shows or shopping for a tractor.

Any of the model-specific books published by *Green* and *Two-Cylinder* magazines. Well-written and very accurate, these books will provide you with the information you need to perform an accurate, original restoration. They usually contain excellent background information about models that can help you choose which model to buy and provide a sense of context to your tractor and your restoration.

Any book by Roger Welsch. None of his books are historical, factual, or specifically about John Deere tractors (in fact, he is partial to Allis Chalmers), but all are funny and entertaining. These books present the lighter side of tractor restoration and collecting.

JOHN DEERE PARTS

The following is a list I have compiled over the years of businesses that more than "dabble" in John Deere tractors. The companies are listed in the categories for which they have the strongest reputation; I've noted if they have products and services and expertise in multiple areas. Also, as with any book, addresses and phone numbers become outdated, so consult periodicals for the latest information. Feel free to drop me a line at jdbook@antique-tractor.com with any corrections, additions, or deletions and I'll try to get them in the next printing of this book. I also remind you that since many of these companies are very small sideline businesses, the owners have other priorities such as a day job or farm work. So, be mindful of the time you call, and be aware of any differences in time zones.

MANUALS

John Deere Distribution Service, 1400 13th Street, East Moline, IL, 61244; (800) 522-7448. This is the best route for buying manuals. Other vendors sell them, but John Deere offers the best quality, the prices are competitive, and it has every manual.

NEW IMPLEMENTS FOR ANTIQUE JOHN DEERE TRACTORS

Tractor Buddies, Inc., PO Box 36, Genesee Depot, WI 53127-0036; (414) 968-9724; Sales@tractorbuddies.com, http://www.TractorBuddies.com. Sells Woods brand implements and mowers that fit antique John Deere tractors.

NOS, NEW, REPRODUCTION, AND SALVAGE PARTS

Agri-Services, 13899 North Road, Alden, NY 14004; (716) 937-6618; http://www.wiringharnesses.com. Wiring harnesses and related supplies.

AGTIQUE Tractor, PO Box 279, Leaf River, IL 61047; (815) 738-2251; http://www.agtique.com. Replacement parts – used and new

Antique Gauges Inc., 12287 Old Skipton Road, Cordova, MD 21625; (410) 822-4963. John Deere-authorized source of replacement gauges; carries other gauges as well.

Nick Barbieri, 4 Monroe Avenue North, Merrick, NY 11566; (516) 221-4116. Reproduction and NOS parts.

John A. Brillman, PO Box 333G, Tatamy, PA 18085; (610) 252-9828. Authentic plug wires and battery cables.

Clarence Bruhn, 2977 Vanderbie Street, St. Paul, MN 55117; summer: (218) 675-6806 or (651) 484-5124. Six-inch lugs for early 1924-1927 D, four-inch lugs for tractor models 1928 and up.

Dave Cook, Route 1, PO Box 25, Washburn, WI 54891; (715) 373-2092. Foot throttle assemblies for 420/430 tractors and crawlers; headlight repair.

Correct Connection, 3345 Copper Kettle Road, Rockwood, PA 15557; (814) 926-2777; corcon@qcol.net. Authentic fasteners for John Deere tractors.

Dengler Tractor & Vintage Tractor Parts Co., 6687 Shurz Road, Middletown, OH 45052; (513) 423-4000; http://www.express-pages.com/d/denglertractor. Lots of rebuilt, reproduction, and used parts; also refaces camshafts and rebuilds carburetors.

Detwiler Tractor Parts, S3266 Highway 13 South, Spencer, WI 54479; (715) 659-4252. New, used, and reproduction parts.

Richard Duane, 311 Congressional Drive, Stevensville, MD 21666; (410) 643-2899. Reproduction grille screens.

General Gear, 733 Desert Wind Rd., Boise, Idaho, 83716 US; (208) 342-8911; http://www.tractorparts.com. Crawlers and antique construction and industrial equipment. This is a great source for crawler information; John Parks, the owner, is extremely knowledgeable.

Dave Geyer, 1251 Rohret Road SW, Oxford, IA 52322; (319) 628-4257. Reproduction hoods for all unstyled tractors.

Green Salvage, Fremont, NC; (919) 242-6154.

Randy Griffith, Letts, IA; (319) 729-5641. Crawler parts, MC through 440.

Corwin Groth, 24880 - 145th Avenue, Eldridge, IA 52738; (319) 285-7009. Reproduction GP parts; GP specialist.

Hart Antique Tractor Reproductions; phone (270) 554-403, Fax: (270) 554-4955; timhart@apex.net. Reproductions of difficult-to-find parts. Reproduction sheet metal for Bs; some for L/LA.

Heritage Farm Power, PO Box 1125, Belton, MO 64012-1125; (816) 474-FARM. Reproduction four- and six-point umbrellas and covers.

IPCO Machine, East Center Street, West Mansfield, OH 43358; (937) 355-4910. Reproduction parts, including top link for Dubuque tractors.

K & K Antique Tractors, 5995 M. 100 West, Shelbyville, IN 46176. John Deere-authorized source of vinyl cut decals.

Stan Knaus, 109 A, 7th, Solomon, KS 67580. Reproduction nickel-plated front hood emblem.

Charles Krekow, 270 - 520th Street, Marcus, IA 51035; (712) 376-2663. For unstyled John Deere Two-Cylinder tractors; reproduction radiator guards and parts to repair your guard.

John R. Lair, 205 A, 6th Street, Canby, MN 56220; (507) 223-5902 (evenings). Like-original fenders for A, B, and G.

Al Larkin, 407 A, Pickwick Drive, Syracuse, IN 46567-1834; (219) 457-4071 (7:00–9:00 p.m. EST). Reproduction round-top fenders for A, B, G, and modified version for H.

Lindstrom's JD Model H Parts, 1275 N.W. 26th Road, St. Joseph, MO 64506; (816) 232-5868 (evenings). One of the premier sources for model H parts.

Marchino M3 Farms Inc., Vincennes, IN 47591; (812) 726-4646. Reproduction flywheels (model A).

Millcreek Valley Farms, 3743 Millcreek Road, Sidney, OH 45365; Reproduction clamshell and flat-top fender brackets.

Phil Miller, 1701 - 480th St. SW, Kalona, IA 52247; (319) 683-2763. Mufflers and reproduction fenders for 430; fender brackets and sway blocks.

Eugene Olson, 1588 V Road, Minden, NE 68959; (308) 832-1679. Reproduction muffler rings and radiator curtains.

Pete's Tractor Salvage, 2163 15th Avenue NE, Anamoose, ND 58710; (800) 541-7383. Very large salvage yard.

Brandon Pfeiffer Tractor Plates, 7810 Upper Mount Vernon Road, Mt. Vernon, IN 47620; (812) 985-2490. Reproduction "BE CAREFUL" plates.

Dennis Polk Equipment, 72435 SR 15, New Paris, IN 46553; (800) 795-3501. Also one of the nation's largest auctioneer of antique farm equipment, and a good source of used John Deere parts.

Gary Polk Equipment, 2990 W. 600 North, Leesburg, IN 46538; (219) 453-2765. Sells new tractors and parts.

Restoration Supply Company, Dept. G, 96 Mendon Street, Hopedale, MA 01747; (508) 634-6915. General restoration supplies and tools

Ridenours, 413 W. State Street, Trenton, OH 45067; (513) 988-0586. John Deere L/LA/LI specialist; also makes reproduction sheet metal.

Rock Valley Tractor Parts, 1004 10th Avenue, Rock Valley, IA 51247; (800) 831-8543. New, used, and rebuilt parts.
Bob Schreiber, 1664 Stone Road, Milo, IA 50166; (515) 466-3393. Reproduction parts.

Leland Schwandt, 14215 468th Avenue, Wilmot, SD, 57279; (605) 432-6192. Specializes in seats, seat parts, and cushions.

Shepard's 2-Cylinder Parts, Service and Repair, E633 1150 Avenue, Downing, WI 54734; (715) 265-4988. Parts, some service and repair.

Tim Sieren, 1320 Highway 92, Keota, IA 52248; (319) 698-4042. Reproduction radiator shutters, and shutter parts and repair.

Steiner Tractor Parts, G-10096 S. Saginaw Road, Holly, MI 48442; (810) 695-1919. Replacement parts; no used or OEM parts.

Stephens Equipment Co., PO Box 89, Frankton, CO 80116; (303) 688-3151. This is one of the largest inventories of NOS John Deere parts in the world. Greg Stephens is a John Deere dealer, and is very knowledgeable and helpful. He regularly writes a column for Green Magazine.

Ed Stoffregen, 19 Warwick Road, Hamilton, OH 45013; (513) 868-0819. Reproduction battery covers and bases for GM tractors. Shutters and smooth covers for A, AR, and B tractors.

Taube Tool Corp., 1524 Chester Blvd., Richmond, IN 47374; http://www.taubetool.com. Polyurethane parade lugs for steel wheels.

Taylor Equipment, 3694 2-Mile Road, Sears, MI 49679; (231) 734-5213. New and used parts.

Tired Iron Salvage, OH; (419) 358-0390. A complete salvage yard with lots of used John Deere parts

2 Cylinder Plus Salvage, Route 2, PO Box 123, Conway, MO 65632; (417) 589-2634. John Deere parts.

Ver Pleog Allied, Inc., 111658 Highway F-62 East, Sulley, IA 50251; (641) 594-4395. Parts, but also sells whole tractors.

Gus Walker, Route 3, PO Box 58, Bloomfield, IA 52537; (515) 459-3476. Used parts.
Levoy Wilcox, {address?} Horace, ND; (701) 281-0398 (after 5:00 p.m. CST). Crawler parts.

Wilson Farms, 20552 Old Mansfield Road, Fredericktown, OH 43019; (740) 694-5071. Used and reproduction sheet-metal parts.

Gary Wolter, 1581 Highway 59, Ocheyedan, IA 51354; (712) 754-2058. Used parts.

RESORATION SERVICES

Automotive Parts & Machine, 900 E. Patrick St. Fredrick, MD 21701; (301) 663-8866. Rebuilds all types of engines, including any tractor engine.

Berns Machinery & Repair, Route 1, PO Box 32A, Blue Hill, NE 68930; (402) 756-3849. Carburetor repair; ask for Karl.

Beyer's Restoration and Shop (Carl Beyer), 26144 Spring Valley Road, Shannon, IL 61078; (815) 864-2153. Complete restorations.

Branson Enterprises, 7722 Elm Avenue, Rockford, IL 61115; (815) 633-4262. Carburetor and magneto restoration.

Dick Buchwoldt, 27404 60th Avenue, Dixon, IA 52745; (319) 843-2270. General restoration of John Deere tractors.

Burrey Carburetor Service, 18028 Monroeville Road, Monroeville, IN 46773; (800) 287-7390.

Kenny Carey, 4889 Plateau Road, Crossville, TN 38555; (931) 277-5227; kcarey@usit.net. Rebuilds DLTX carburetors and Wico magnetos; will pick up and deliver; complete restorations.

Central Fuel Injection, 2409 Murray Road, Estherville, IA 51334; (712) 362-2212; http://www.ncn.net/~edco/edco.html. Rebuilt diesel injection pumps and nozzles.

Denny's Carburetor Shop, 8620 N. Casstown-Fletcher Road, Fletcher, OH 45326; (937) 368-2304. Also sells solid-state ignitions.

Geigle Repair, 571 S. Downey Street, Walcott, IA 52773; (319) 284-6655. Magneto repair.

"GP" Specialist Corwin Groth, 24880 - 145th Avenue, Eldridge, IA 52748; (319) 285-7009. Call or send for list of rebuilding services that includes carburetors, magnetos, spark arrestor mufflers, steering rebuilds, and so on. Completely restores GP series tractors.

Joe's Auto Body, 11807 Lax Chapel Road, Kiel, WI 53042; (920) 894-2134. Restoration services.

John's Machine and Diesel Repair, 226 Main, Milan, MN 56262; (320) 734-4441. Engine (complete) machine shop service.

Jungmeyer Tractor Restoration Service, 55835 Highway C, Russellville, MO 65074; (573) 782-4602.

Ken's Body Shop, 124 East Cleveland Road, Huron, OH 44839; (800) 843-2395.

Mark Ketron, Route 1, PO Box 424-A, Lebanon, VA 24266; (540) 880-1298 (6:00–9:00 p.m. EST). Tractors, crawlers, implements; will pick up and deliver; complete restorations.

Earl Lundin, Route 1, PO Box 73, Revillo, SD 57259; (605) 678-2694. Carburetor and magneto repair.

MacDonald Carb and Ignition, 1001 Commerce Road, Jefferson, GA 30549; (706) 367-8851.

Mag-Electro Service (Glen Schueler), 300 FM 2013, Friona, TX 79035; (806) 295-3682.

Magneeders, Route 5, PO Box 505, Carthage, MO 64836; (417) 358-7863. Magneto restoration services.

Magneto Repair; 800-MAG-NETO. Magneto restoration services.

Minn-Kota Repair (Murlyn Schnaser), Route 1, PO Box 243, Ortonville, MN 56278; (320) 289-2473 or (320) 839-3940. Recovers steering wheels; reproduction rubber torsion seat springs, eye bolts, PTO covers, radiator caps, radiator flange fillers, and more.

Nielsen Spoke Wheel Repair (Bernard "Herb" Nielsen), 3921 - 230th Street, Estherville, IA 51334; (712) 867-4796. Spoke wheel repair.

Paper Pulleys, Inc., 810 Woodland Street, Columbia, TN 38402; (931) 388-9099. Restores paper core belt pulleys.

Dennis Polk & Associates, 72435 SR 15, New Paris, IN 46553; (800) 795-3501; parts@dennispolk.com, www.dennispolk.com, or http://www.auctionpage.net. RAM Remanufacturing and Distributing, Inc., N. 604 Freya, Spokane, WA 99202; (800) 233-6934; RAMRemfg@aol.com,

http://members.aol.com/RAMRemfg/Home/sales.html. The vintage Engine Machine Works Division can complete any type of engine machining you need for your antique tractor, including most babbitting work.

Red Oak Diesel Clinic, 2500 N. Fourth Street, Red Oak, IA; phone (712) 623-2221, Fax (712) 623-3808. Repairs and services diesel engines and fuel systems; full-line support service program available.

Renaissance Tractor, 120 Cabe Road, Chehalis, IA 98532; (800) 784-0026 or (360) 748-0026. Diesel fuel-injection repair and recalibration; block boring; block, piston, injector packages available.

Robert's Carburetor Repair, PO Box 624, Spencer, IA 51301; (712) 262-5311. Also sells videos on how to do it yourself.

Rusty Acres (the Petermans), 1057 180th Street, Webster City, IA 50595; (515) 543-8641; rstyrest@wccta.net. Complete restorations.

Schultz Gas Engines (Lyle Schultz), Route 1, PO Box 31-A, Chatfield, MN 55923; (507) 867-3442. Most tractor models (1925 D 820), including magneto and carburetor repair; complete restorations.

Sindt Implement, Keystone, IA; (800) 568-4461. Repair and mechanical work.

Speigelberg Restoration, P.O. Box 63 Birmingham, OH 44816; (440) 965-7679; http://www.srstractor.com. Expo-quality restorations; a lot of his work appears in this book.

Tim Talbot, 3619 Johnson Street Road, Keokuk, IA 52632; (319) 524-8383. Complete restorations and starter and generator rebuilding.
Tractor Steering Wheel Recovering and Repair, 1400 121st Street W, Rosemount, MN 55068; (651) 455-1802. Steering-wheel recovering.

Triple "G" Service, 12056 Buckwheat Road, Alden, NY 14004; (716) 542-3175. Complete mechanical services.

2 Cylinder Diesel Shop, Route 2, PO Box 241, Conway, MO 65632; (417) 589-3843. Specializes in John Deere Two-Cylinder diesel engines.

2-Cylinder Repair and Sales (Gary Schmitt), 22040 190th Street, Rockwell, IA 50469; (641) 822-4662. Complete restorations and rebuilds; also has parts.

Gary Uken, 1909 - 330th Street, Titonka, IA 50480; (515) 928-2010. Expo-quality restorations—some of his work appears in this book; he also writes a regular column for Two-Cylinder Magazine.

Brian Vickers, 7801 Cedar Island Road, Omaha, NE 68147; (402) 734-7452; trcolman@aol.com. Complete restorations, machine work, and engine rebuilding.

Mike Williams, 206 - 32nd Avenue North, Clinton, IA 52732; phone (319) 243-4928, Fax (319) 243-3065. Rebuilds tapered splines on crankshafts to factory specs for A, B, G, etc.; reproduces wide-front upright shafts with correct taper splines; reproduces nearly any gear, bushing, shaft, or linkage, including camshafts and rocker shafts; rebuilds worn housings, bores holes, drawbars, etc., to new specs; repairs, rebuilds, or reproduces most fuel tanks. Mike's work appears in this book.

RESTORATION SUPPLIES AND TOOLS

Jorde's Decals, 935 9th Avenue NE, Rochester, MN 55906; (507) 288-5483. Very highly regarded source for John Deere decals.

Lubbock Gasket and Supply, 402 19th Street, Lubbock, TX 79401; (800) 527-2064. Custom and standard gaskets for antique tractors.

POR 15 Inc., PO Box 1235, Morristown, NJ 07962; (800) 576-5822; http://www.por15.com. The gas tank sealing kit is especially effective.

Joe Sykes, 935 - 9th Avenue NE, Tonawanda, NY 14150; (716) 691-8519. Custom-made piston rings—any size.

TIP, PO Box 649, Canfield, OH 44406; (800) 321-9260. Very nice selection of quality sandblasting products.

TIRES

M. E. Miller Tire, 17386 State Highway 2, Wauseon, OH 43567; (419) 335-7010. Also sells memorabilia, tire putty, and parade lugs.

Tucker's Tire, 844 S. Main Street, Dyersburg, TN 38024; (800) 443-0802.

HAULING AND SHIPPING SERVICES FOR TRACTORS

B&B Custom Hauling (Brian Block), MT; (406) 549-4418 or (406) 360-3636. Tractor transportation and trucking.

Moore Bros. Trucking, Inc., 12140 Slopertown Road, Davenport, IA 52804; (800) 642-3097. Tractor transportation and trucking.

Index

Antique Tractor Bible
0-7603-0335-5

**How to Rebuild and Restore
Farm Tractor Engines**
0-7603-0661-3

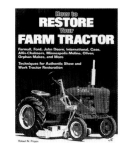

**How to Restore Your
Farm Tractor**
0-8793-8593-6

**How to Restore
Tractor Magnetos**
0-8793-8949-4

**John Deere Two-Cylinder
Collectibles**
0-7603-0750-4

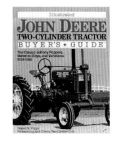

**John Deere
Two-Cylinder Tractor**
0-8793-8659-2

John Deere Collectibles
0-7603-0830-6

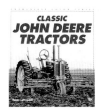

Classic John Deere Tractors
0-8793-8865-X

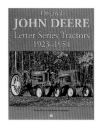

**Original John Deere
Letter Series Tractors
1923-1954**
0-7603-0912-4